Monster Truck Drawing Book

We hope you liked this drawing book.

Please leave a review or feedback to help us create a better product for you.

Thank you for your love and support !!!

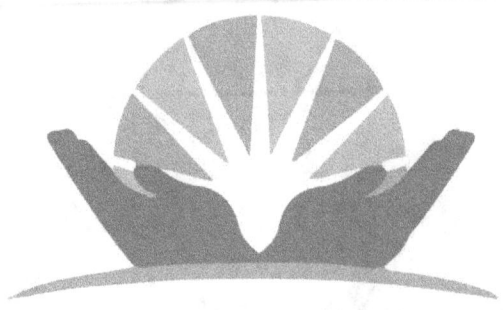

I AM CREATIONS LLP

Copyright © 2021 All Rights Reserved

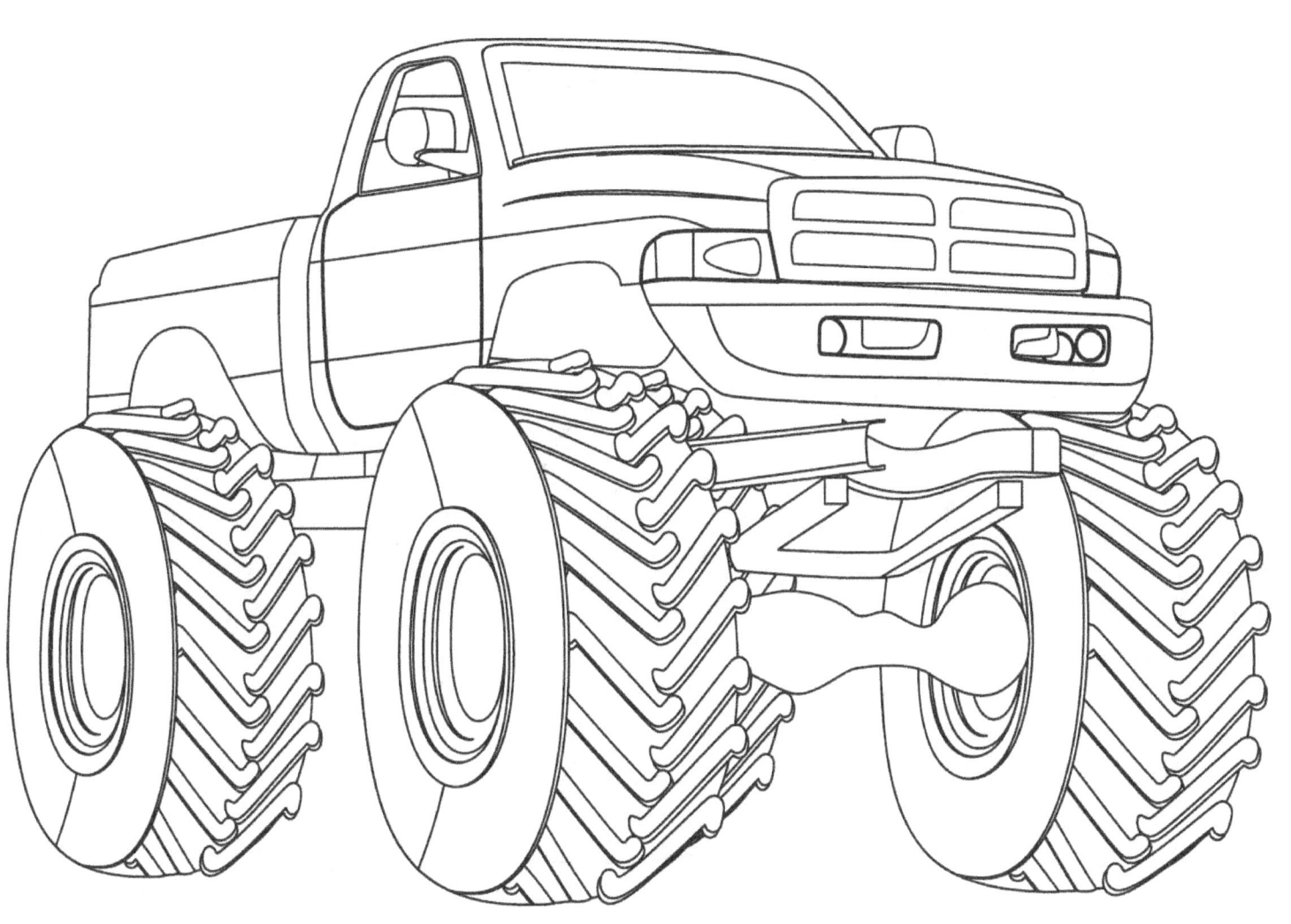

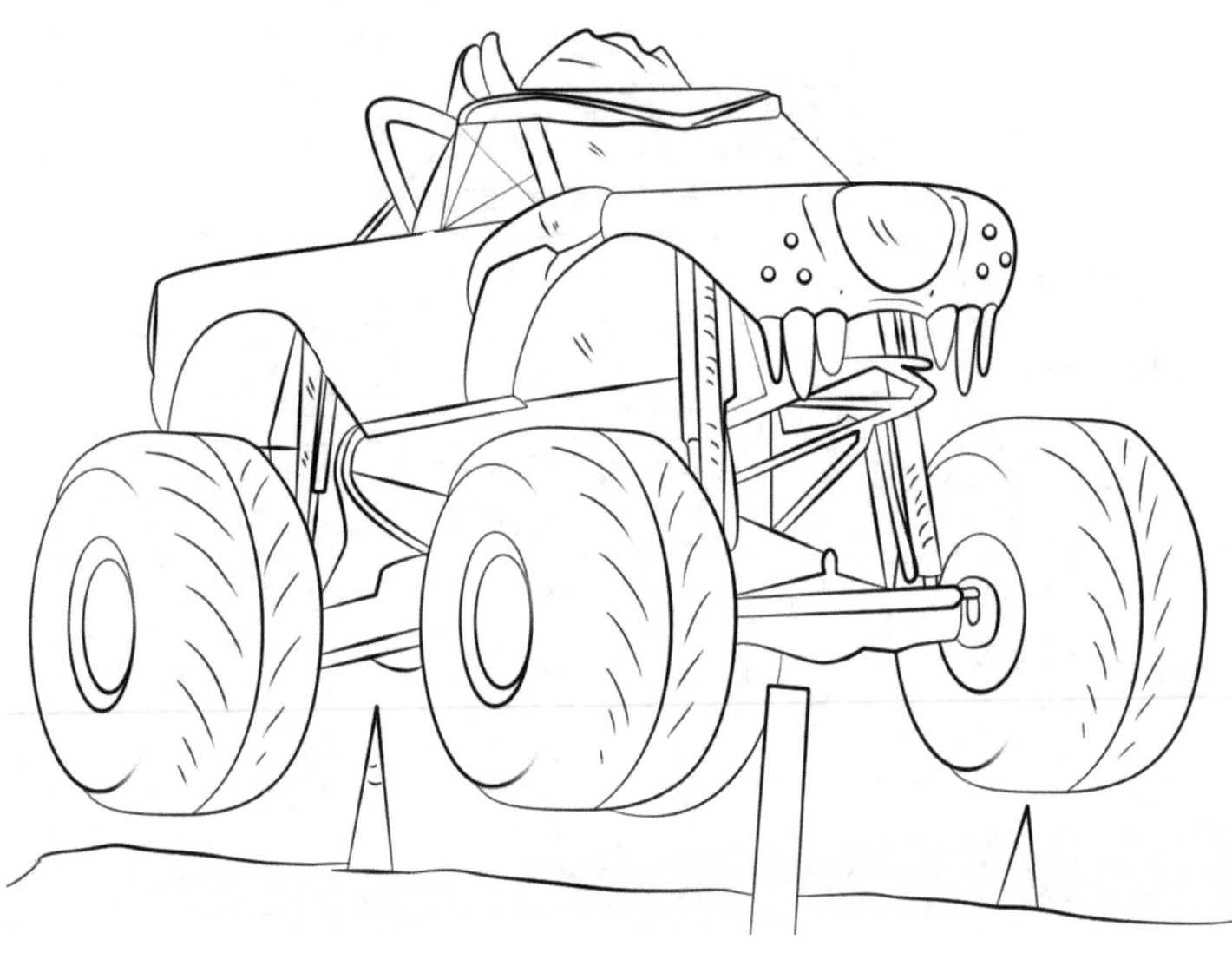

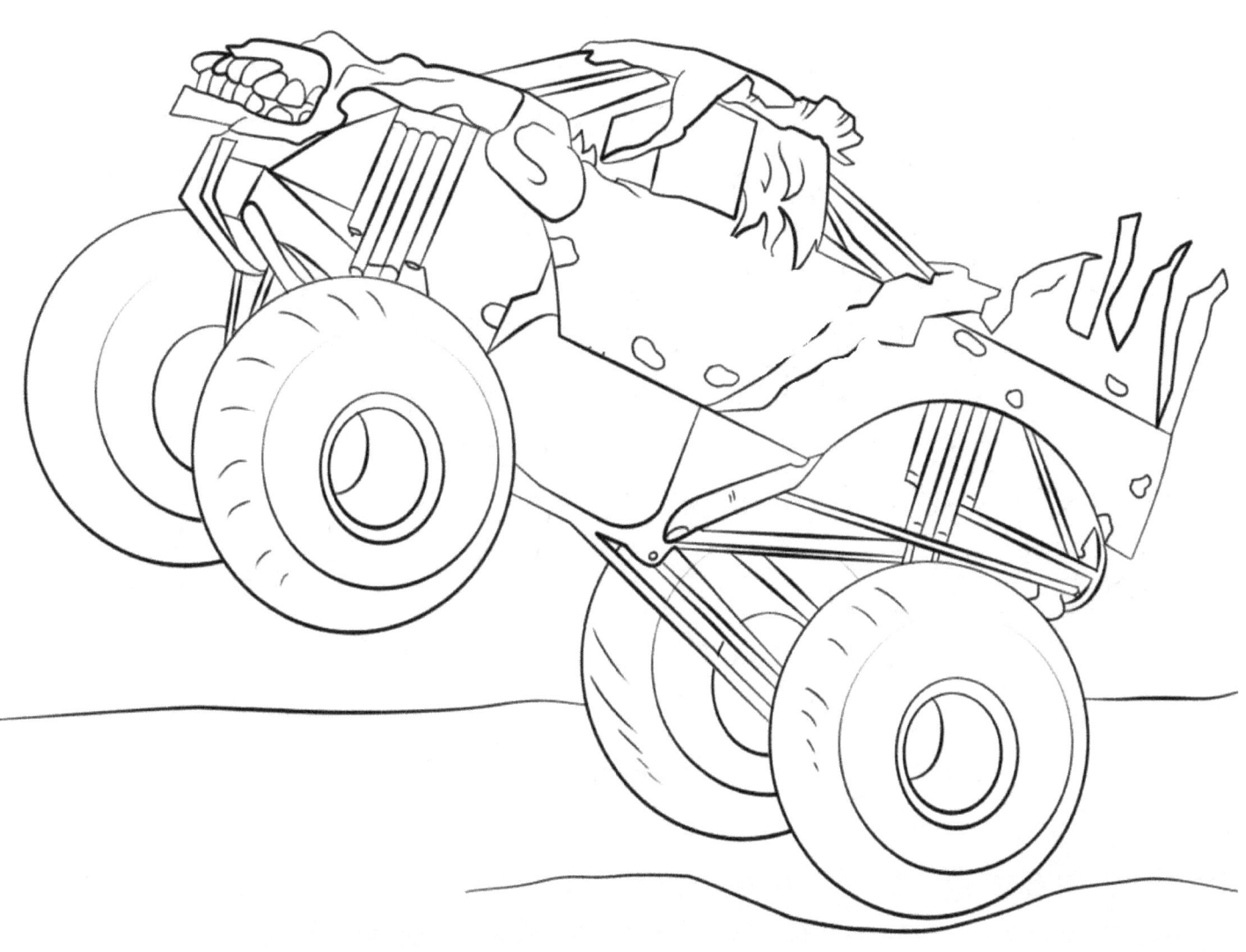

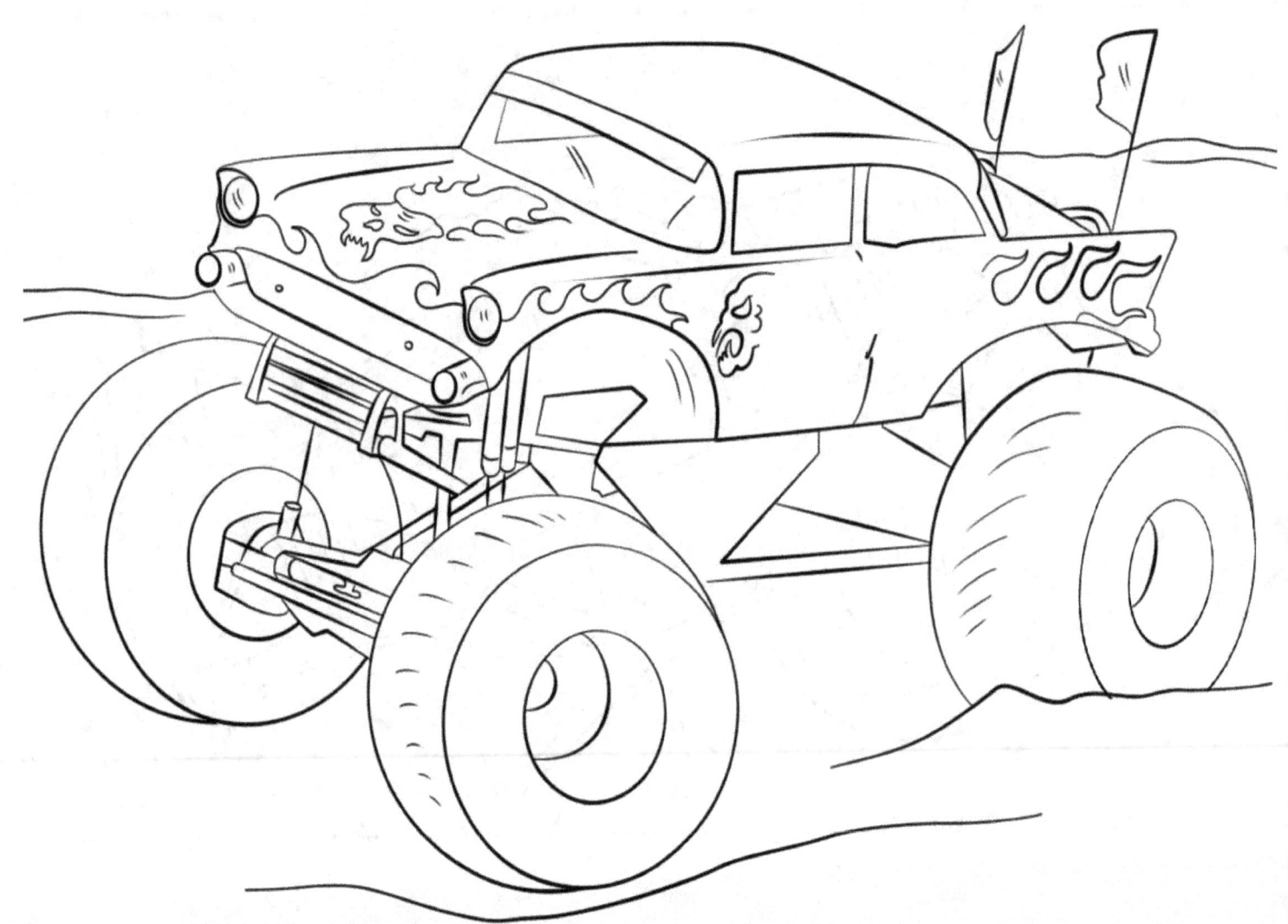

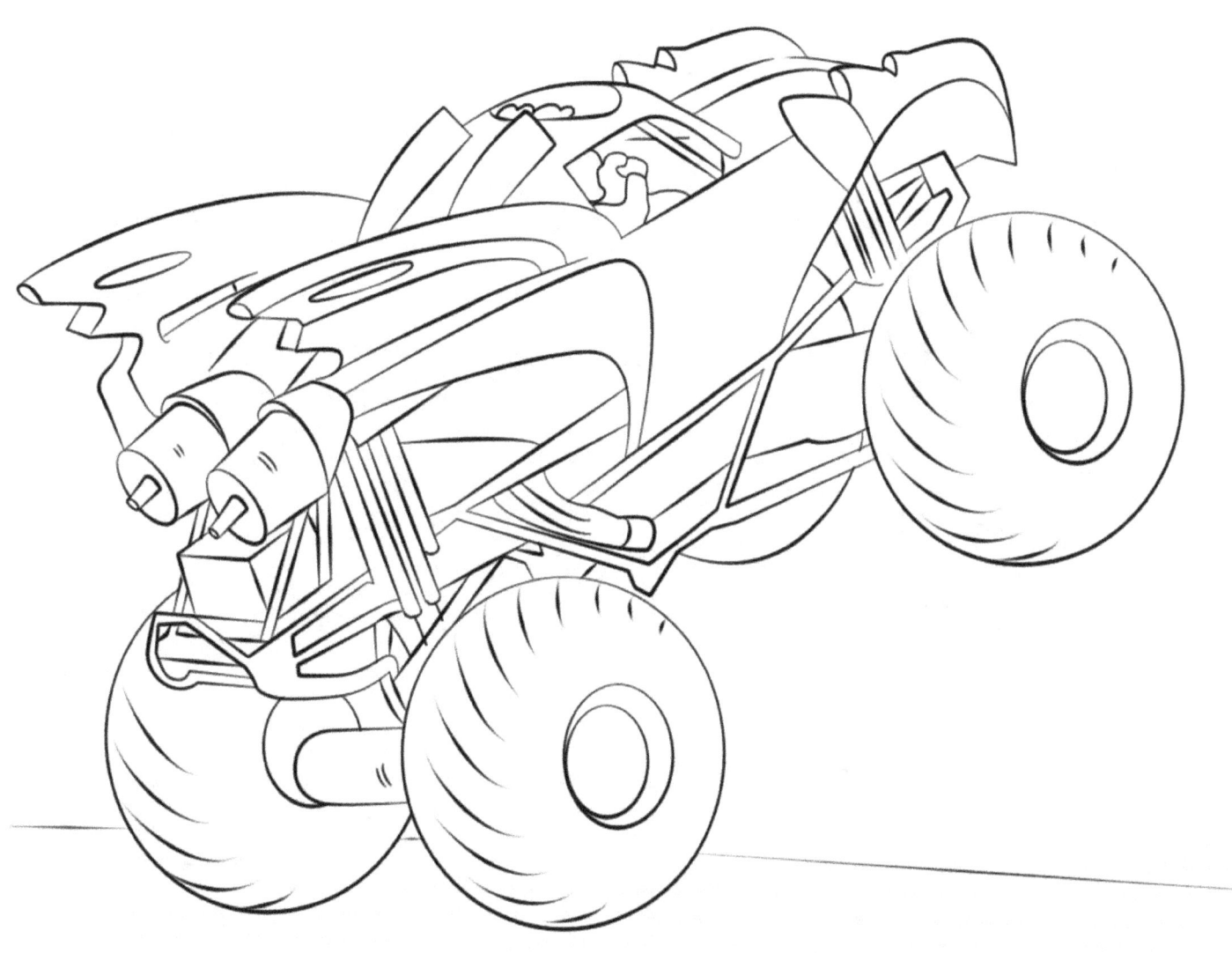

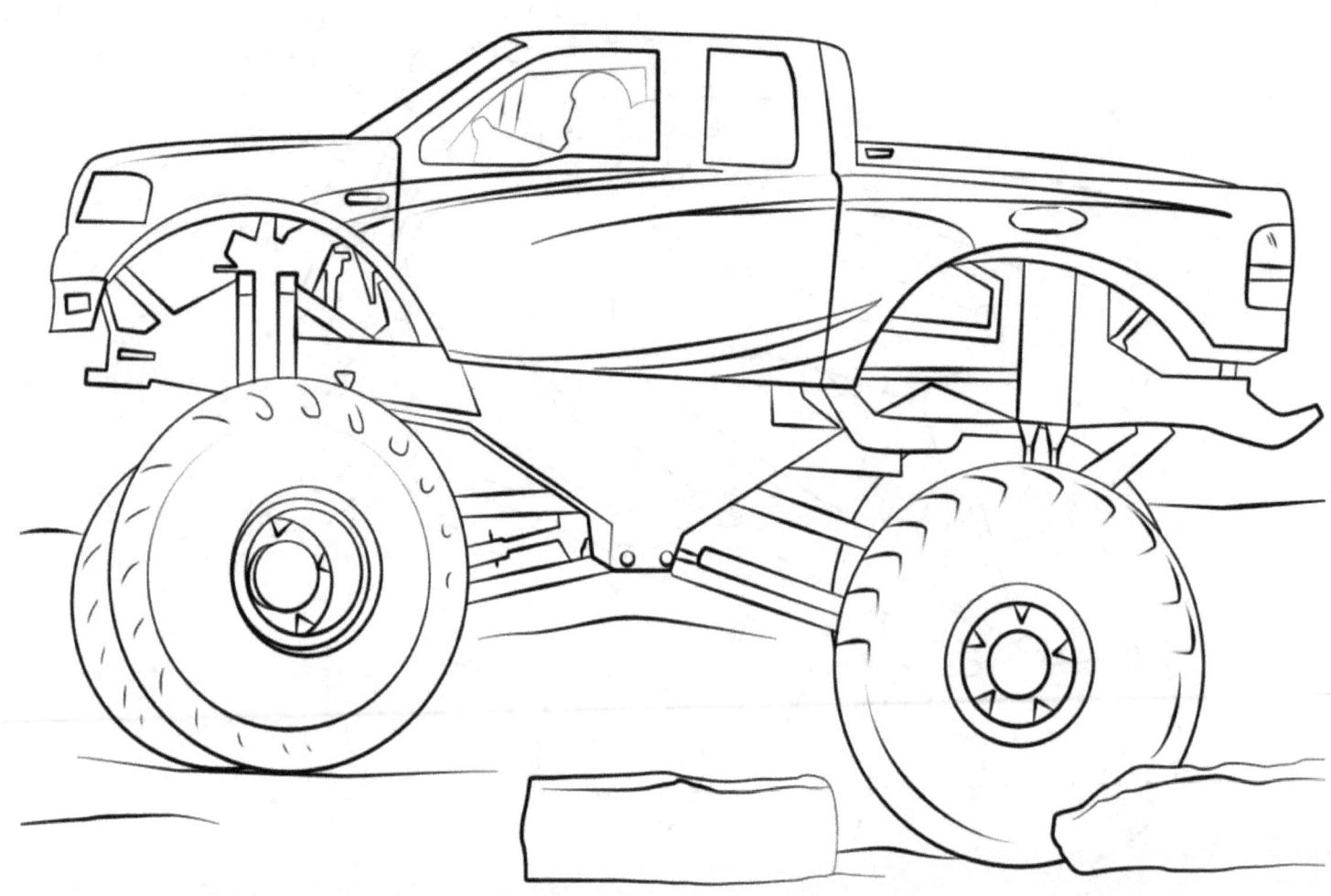

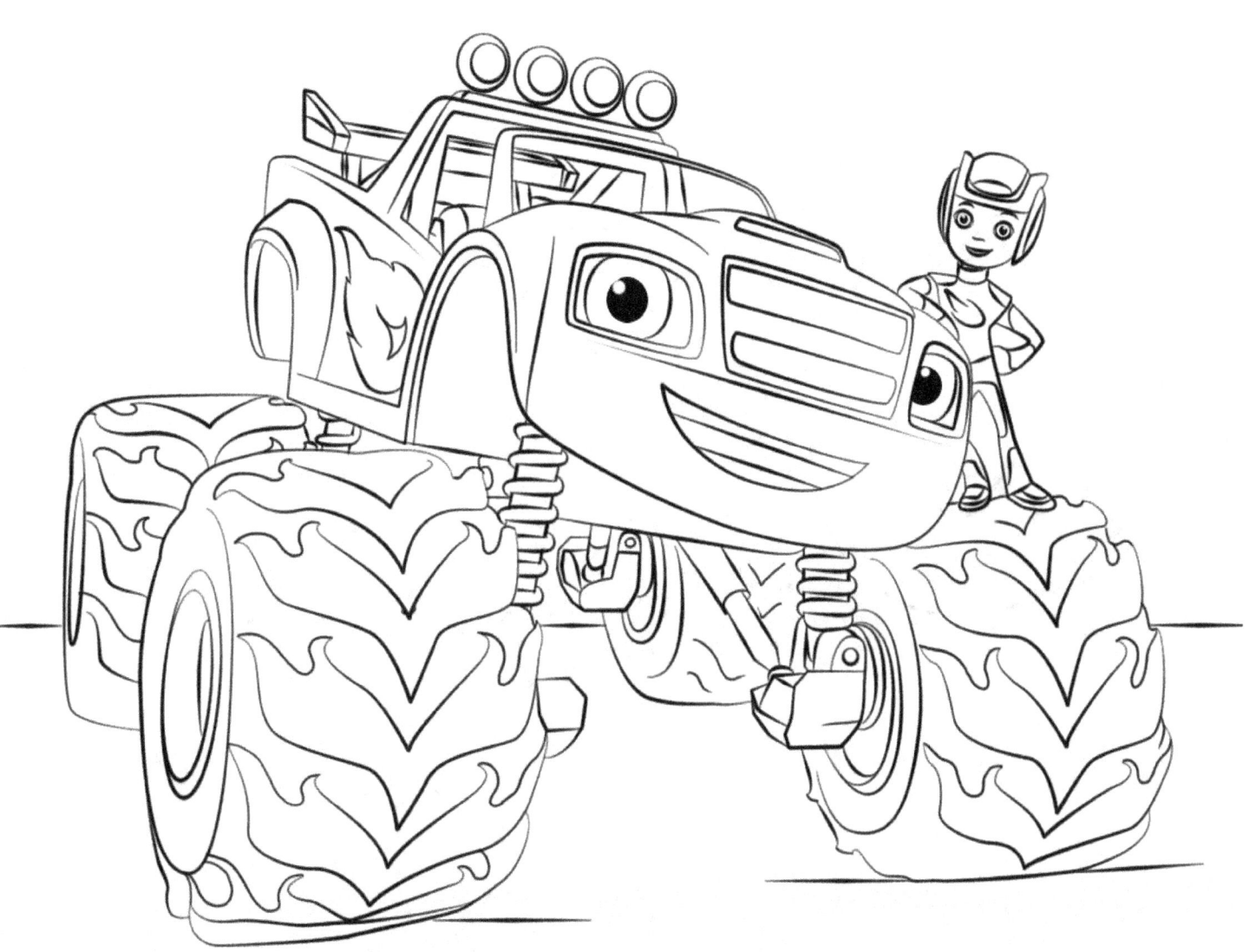

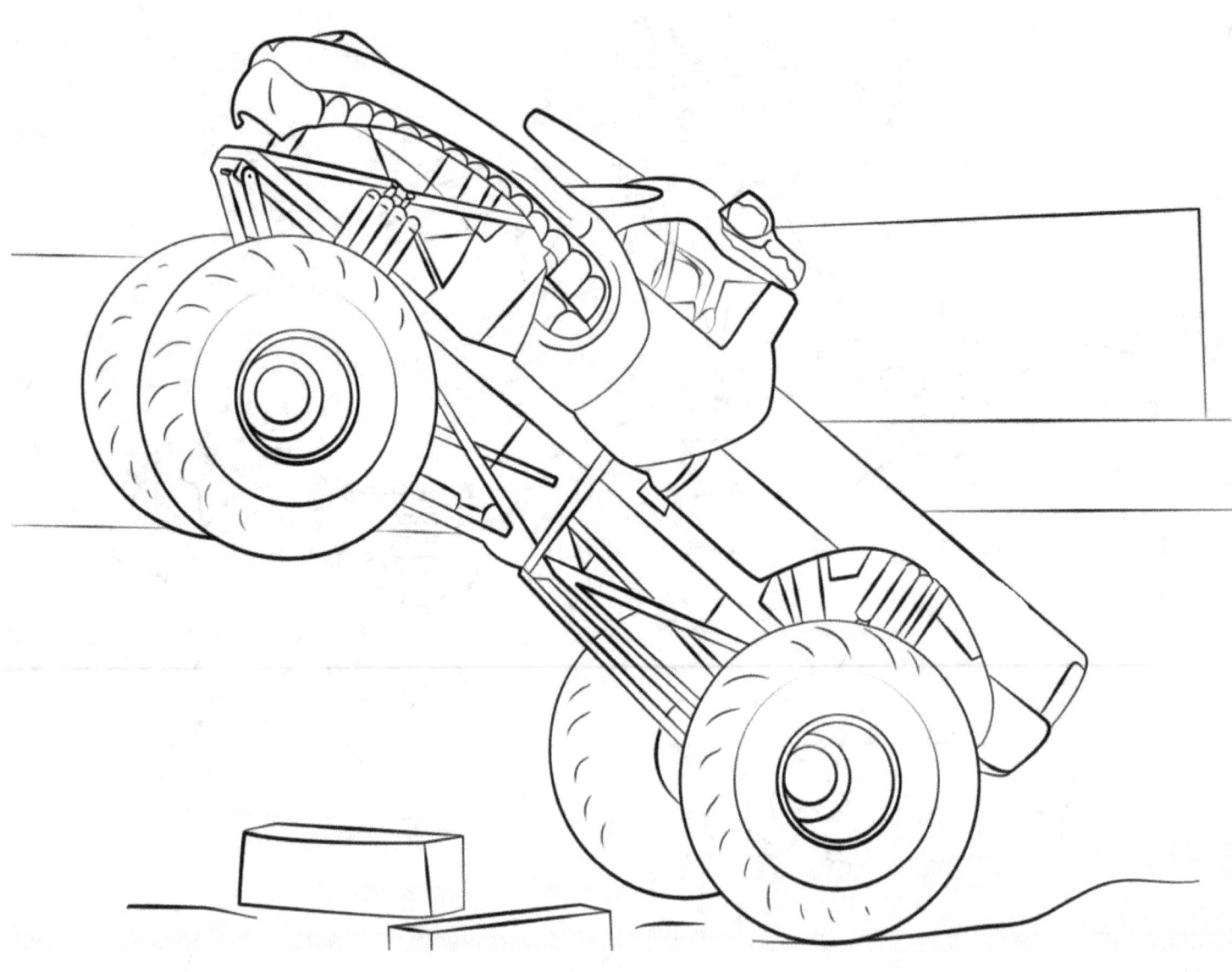

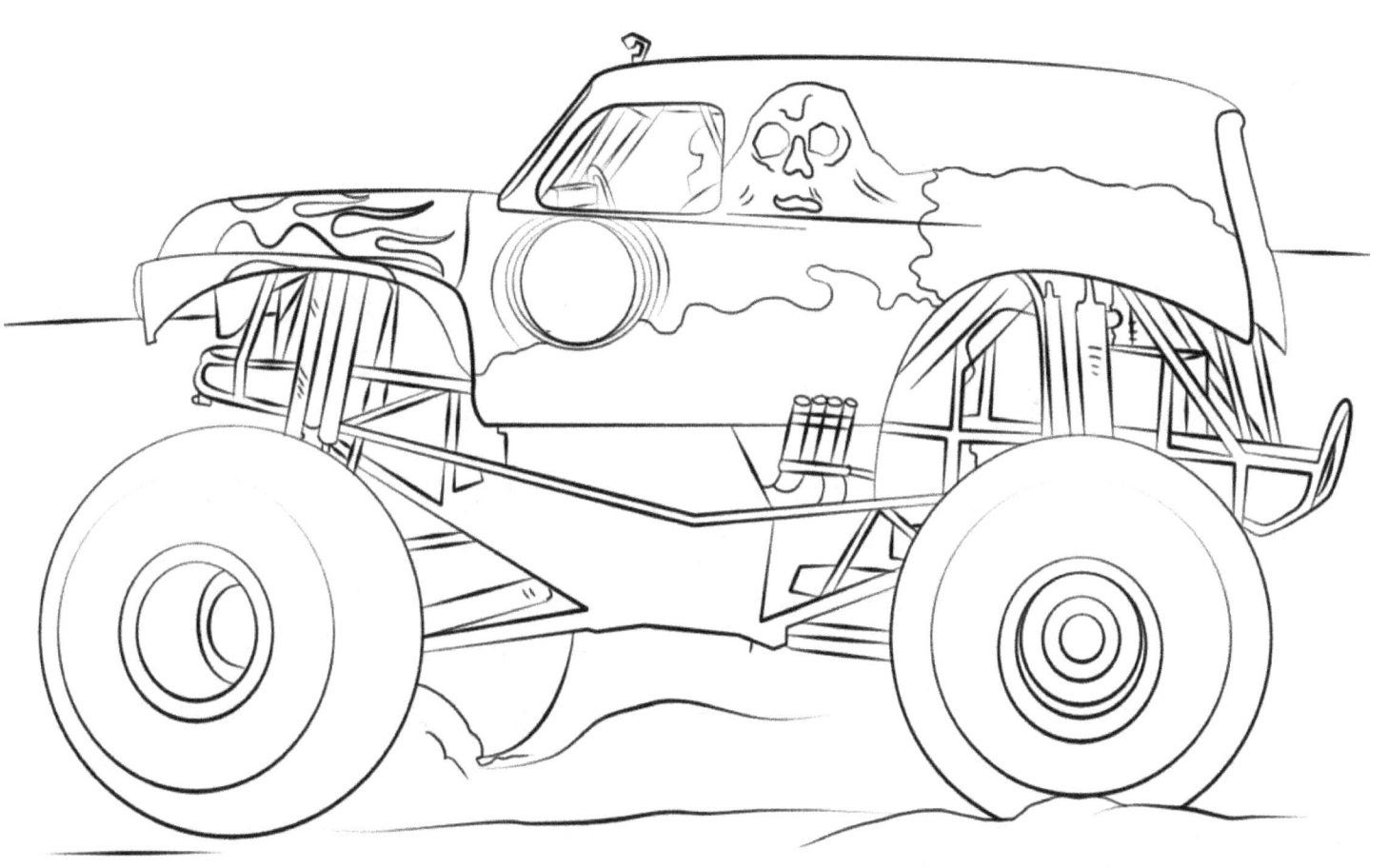

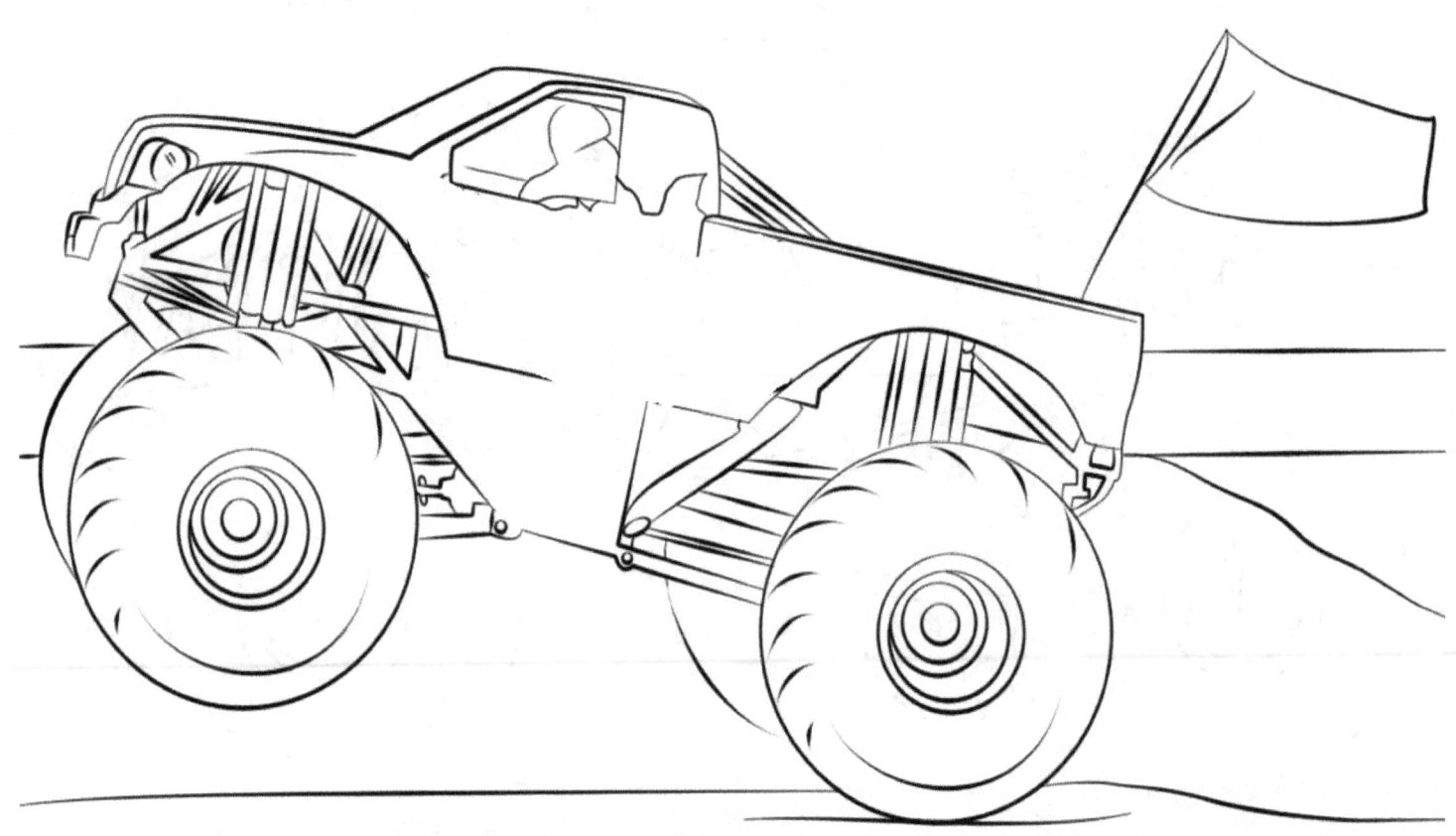

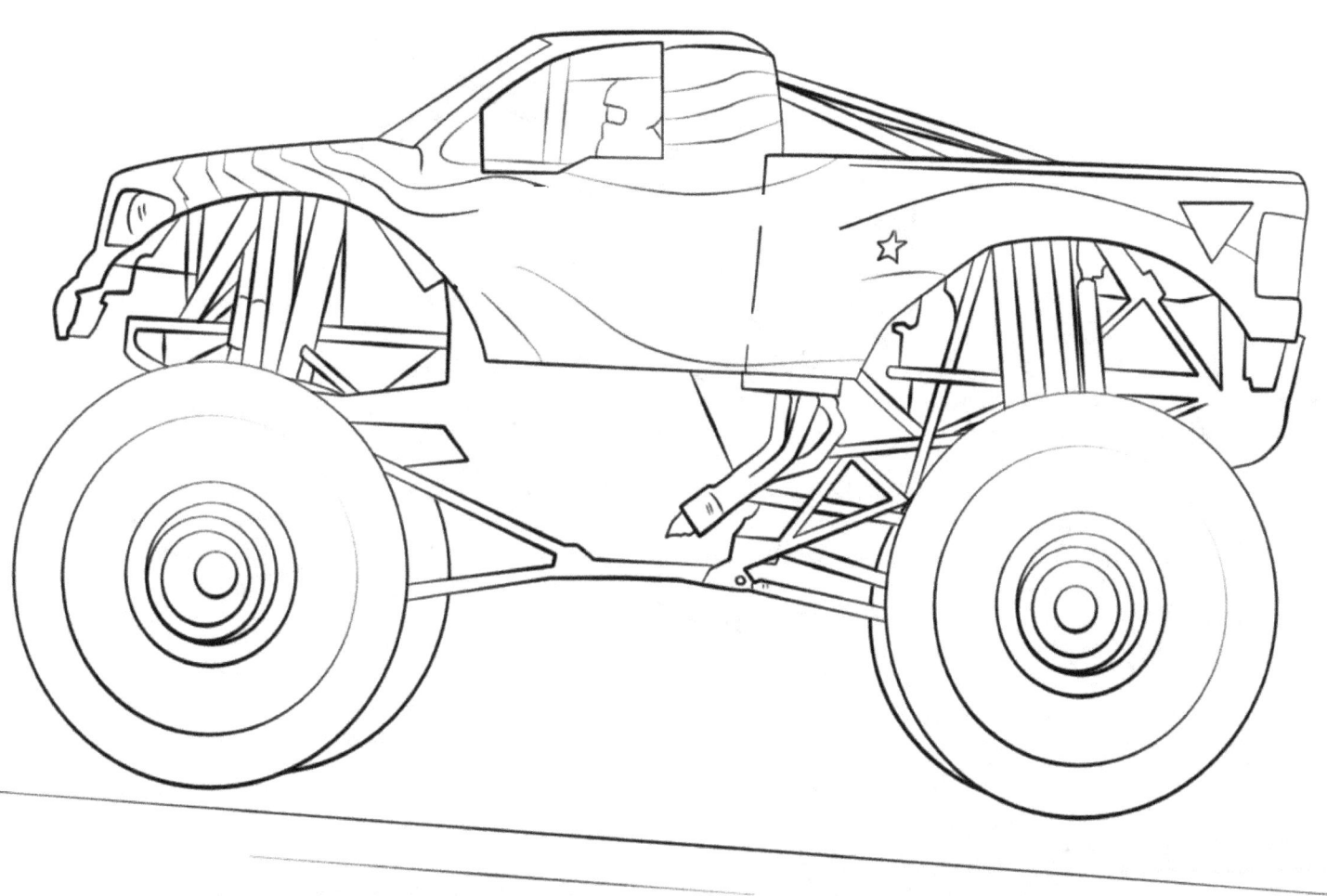

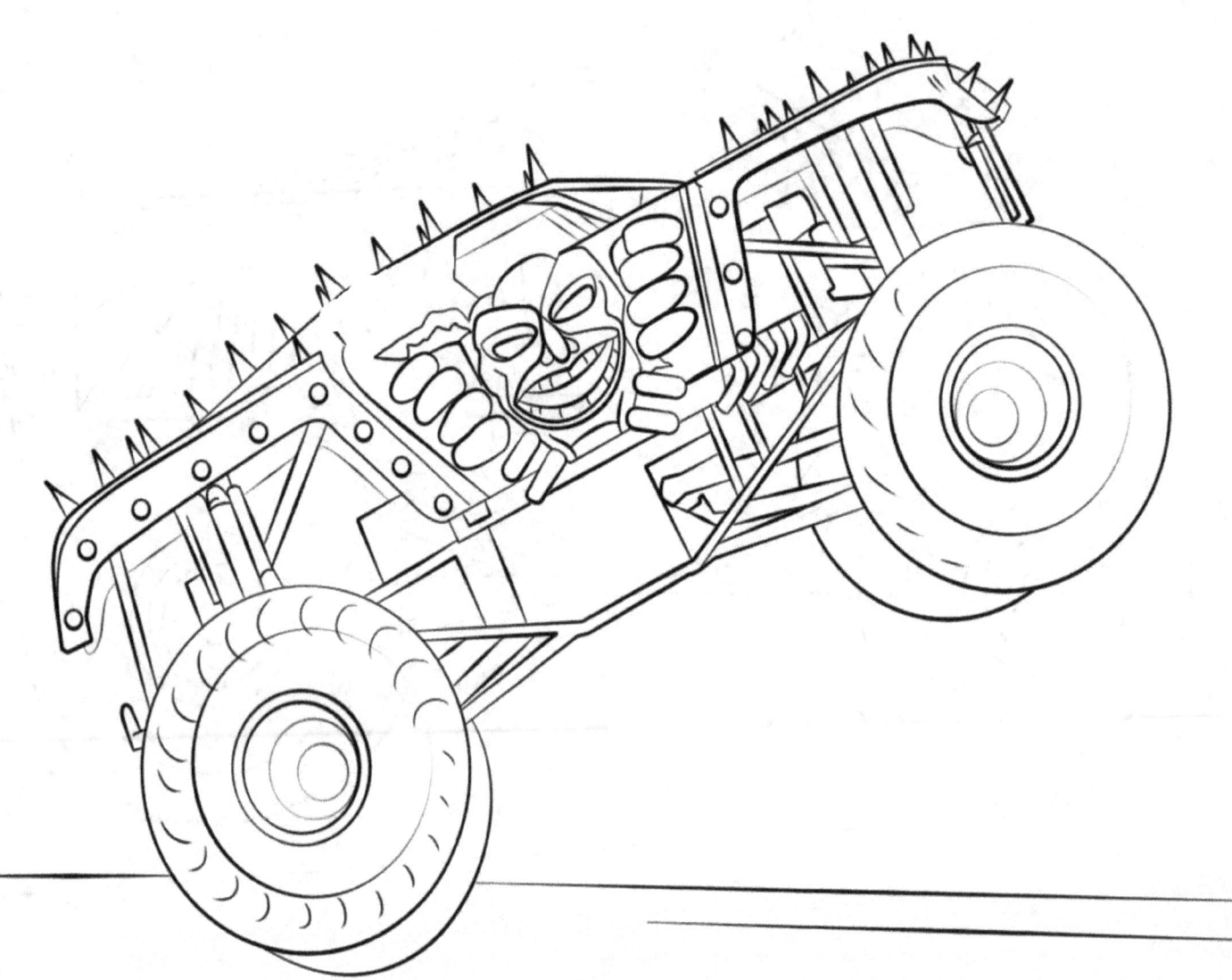

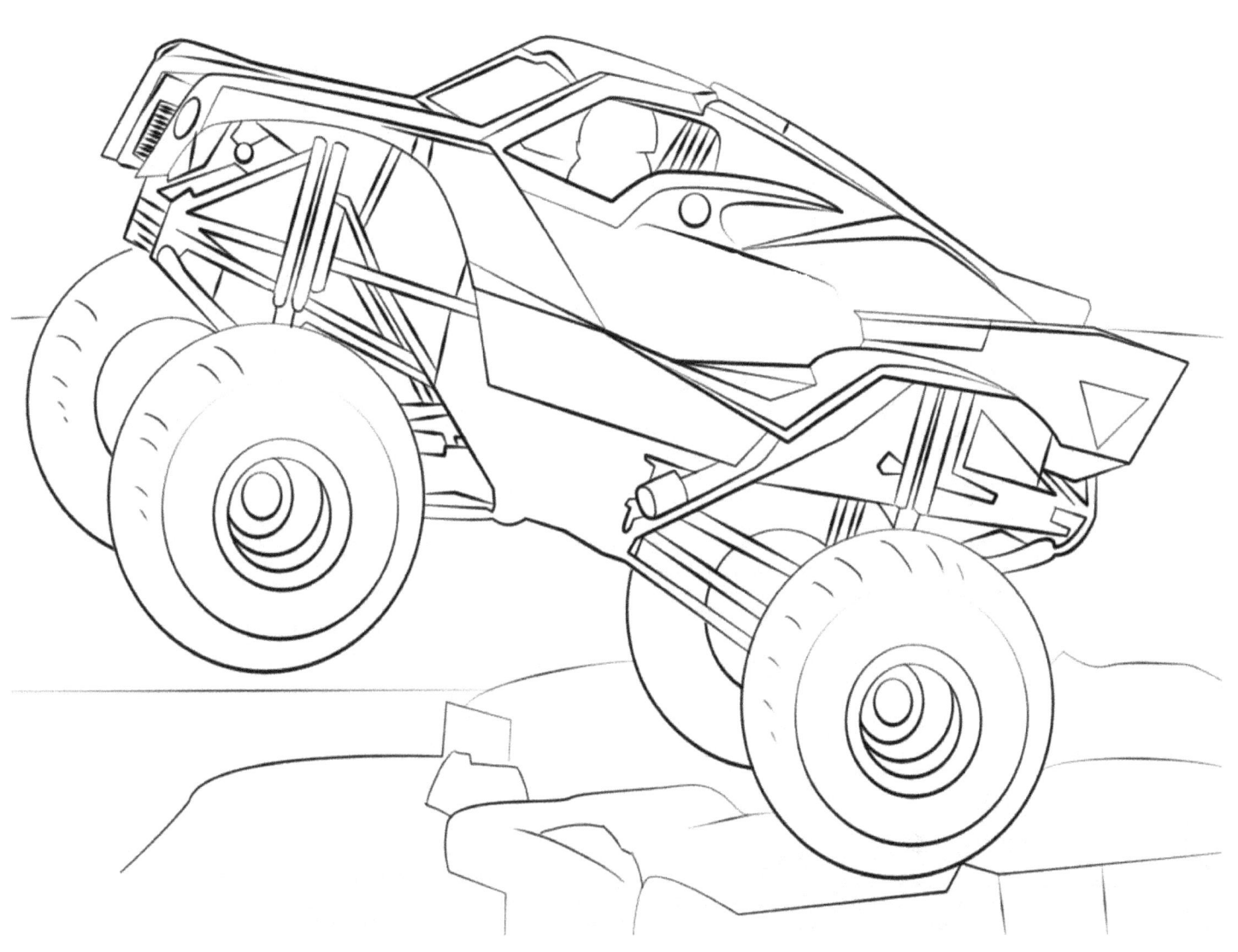

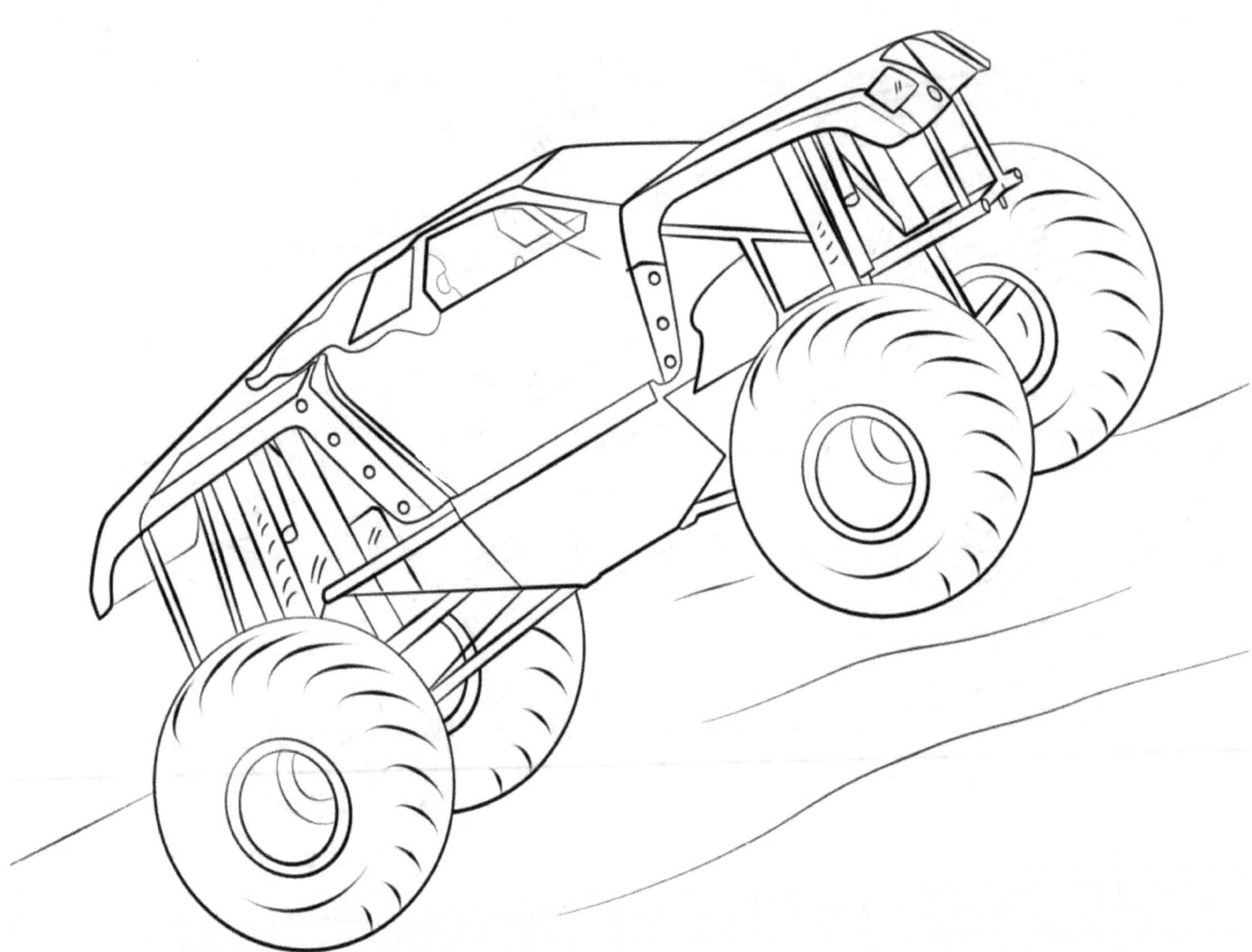

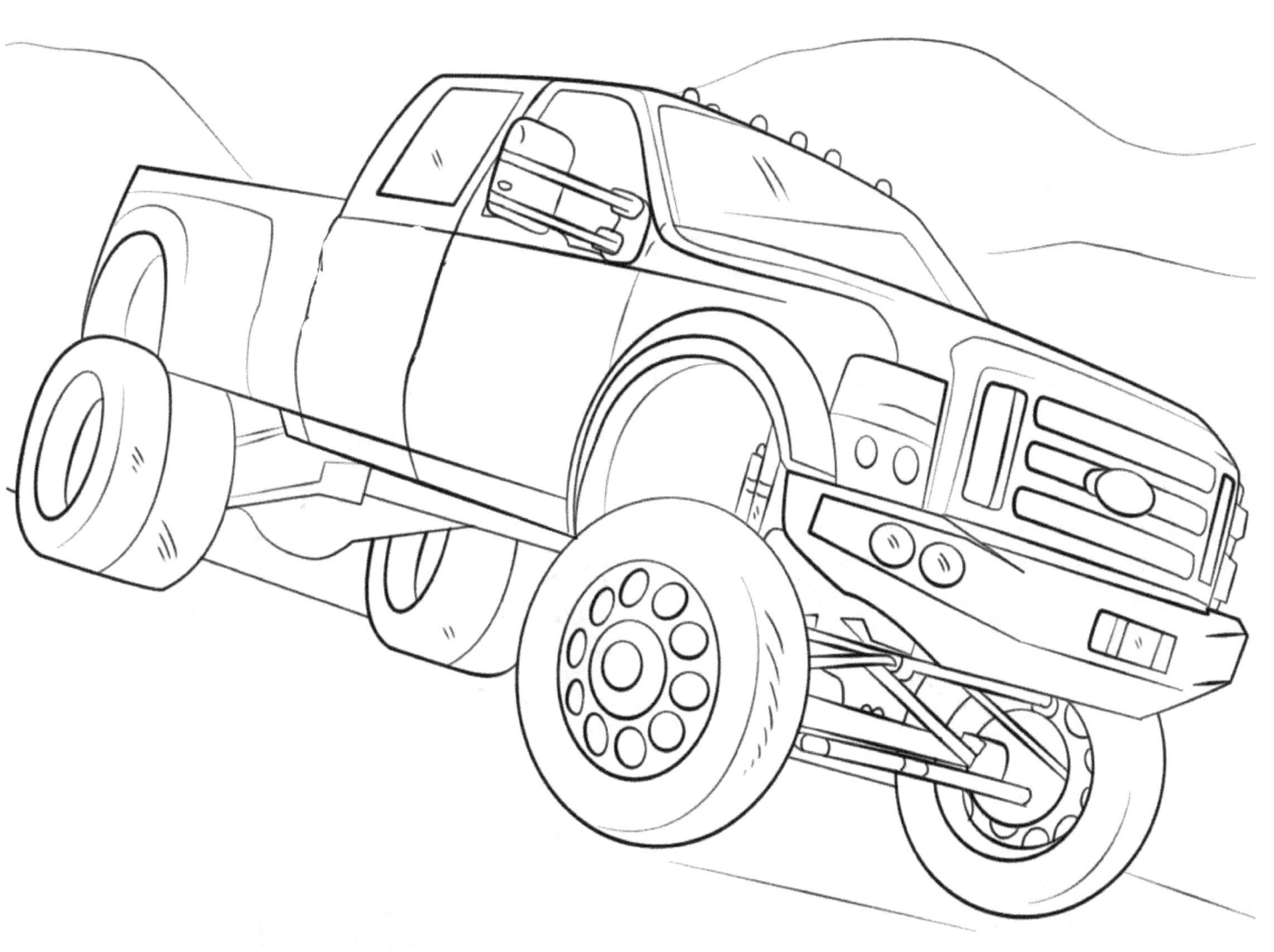

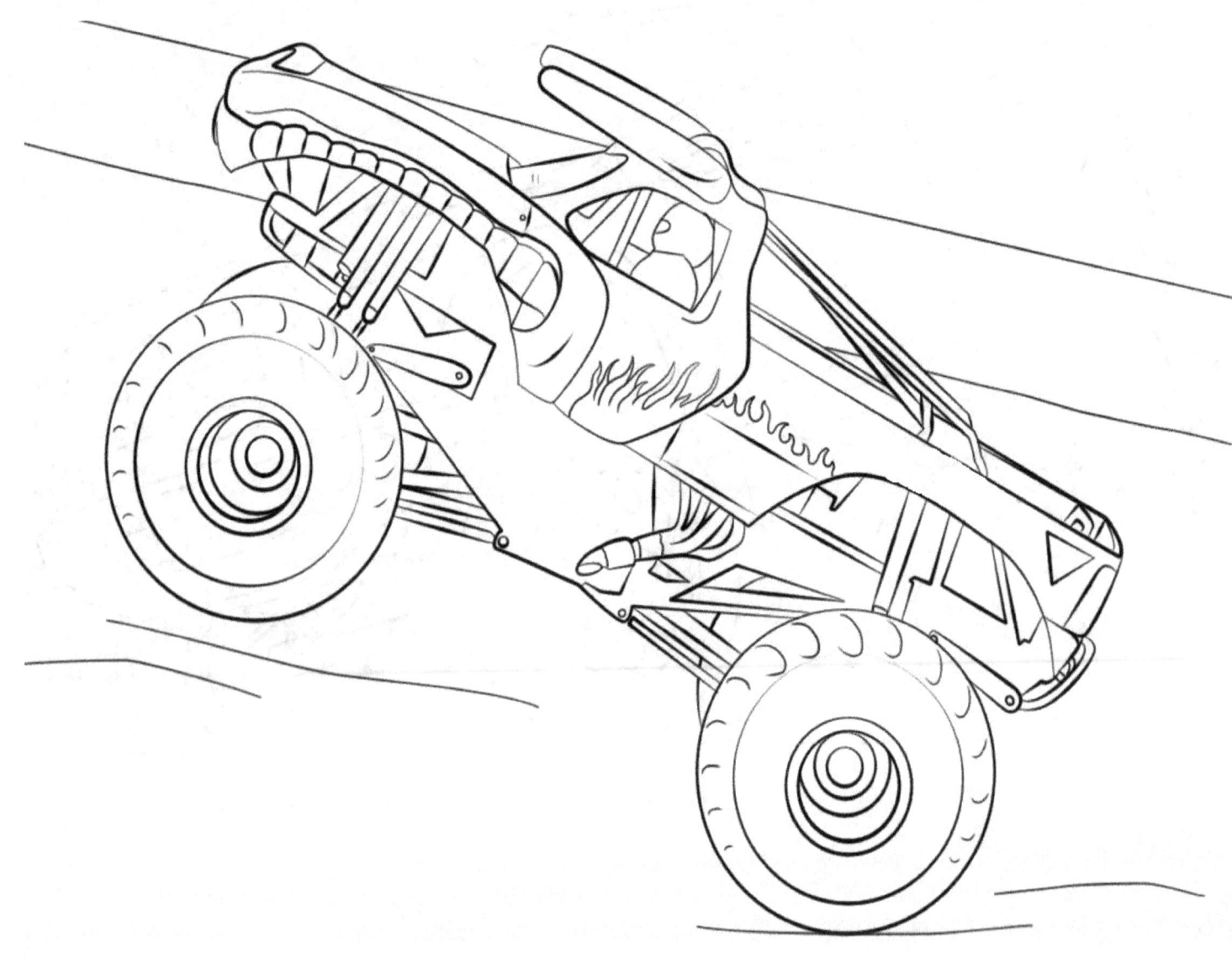

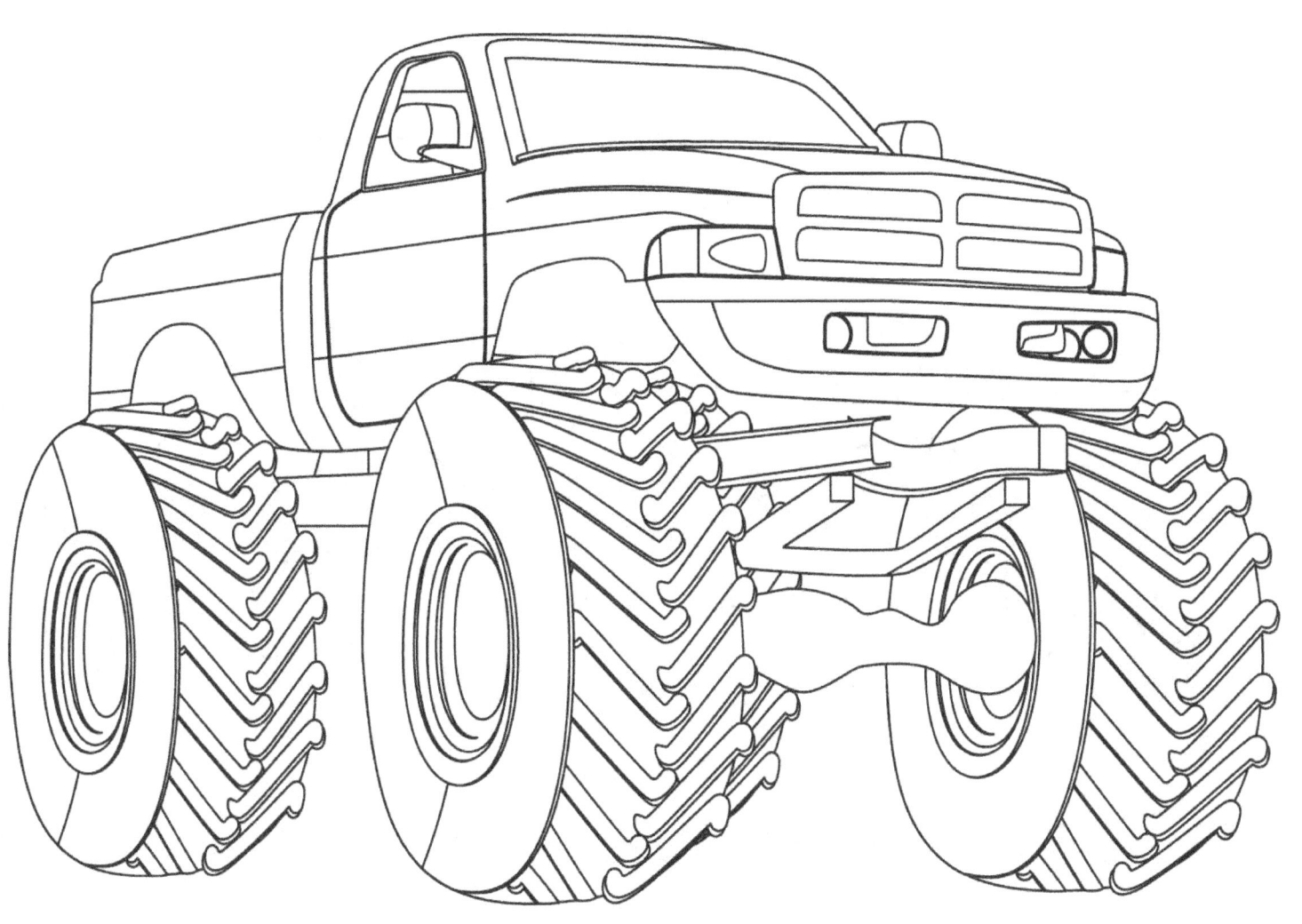

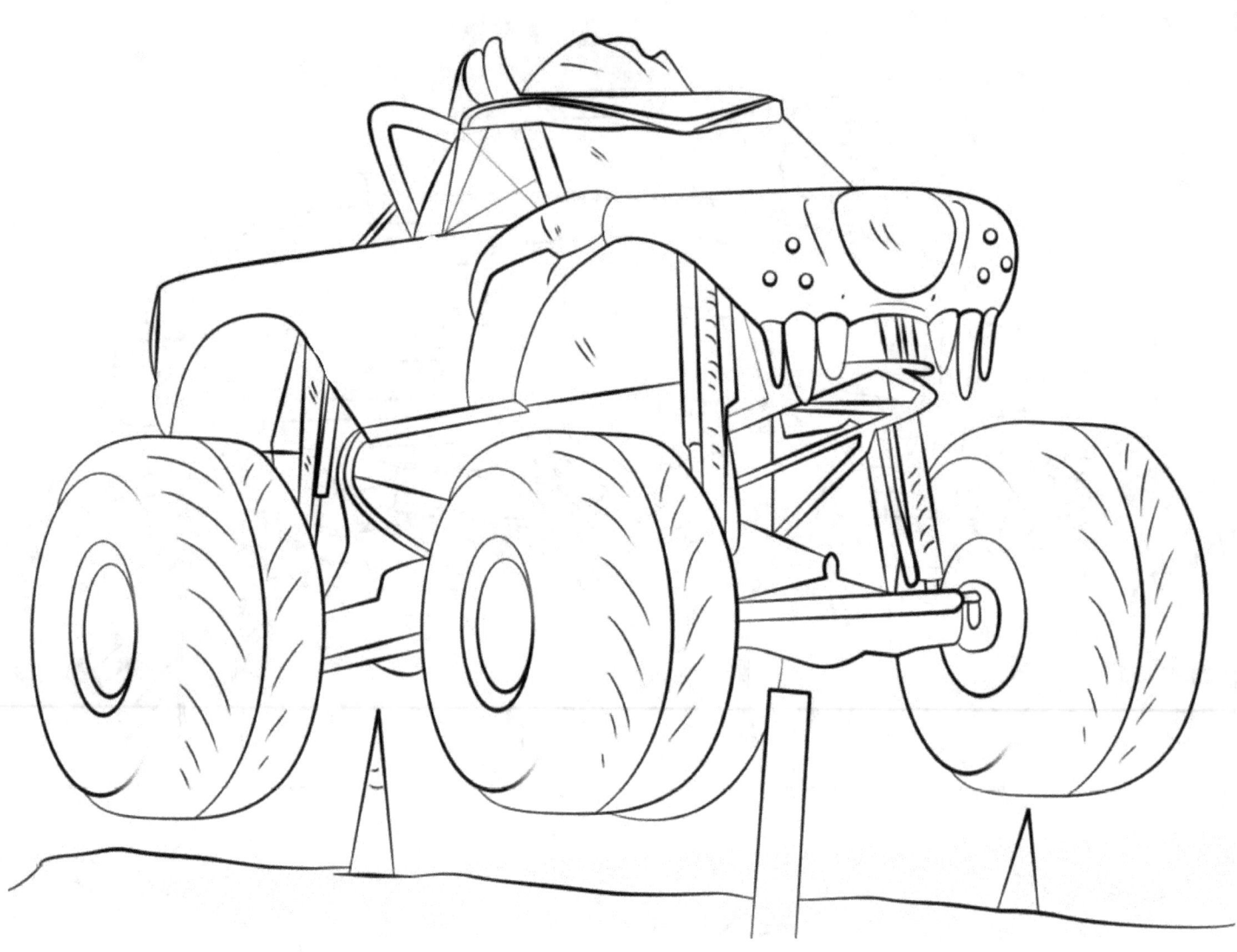

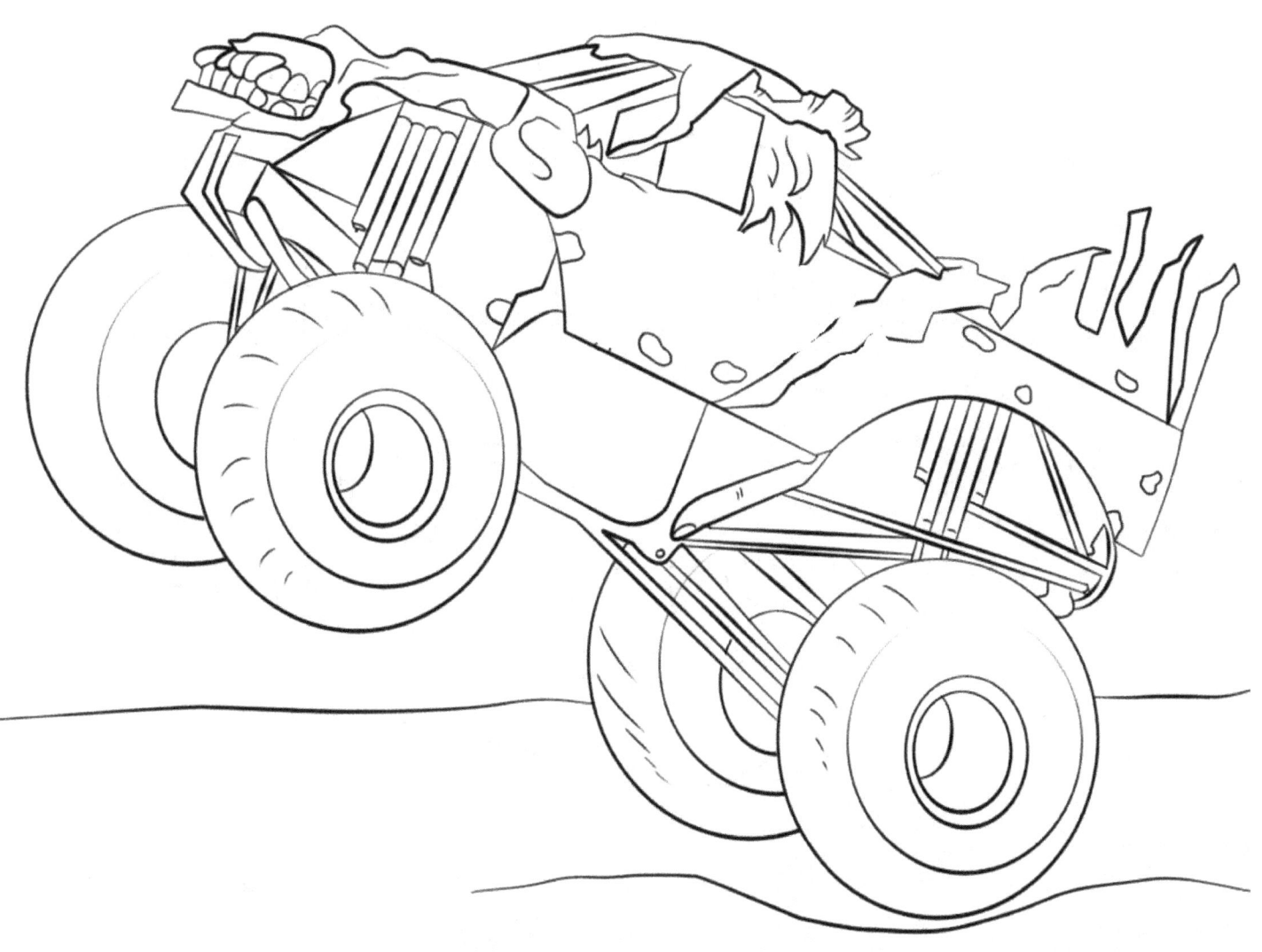

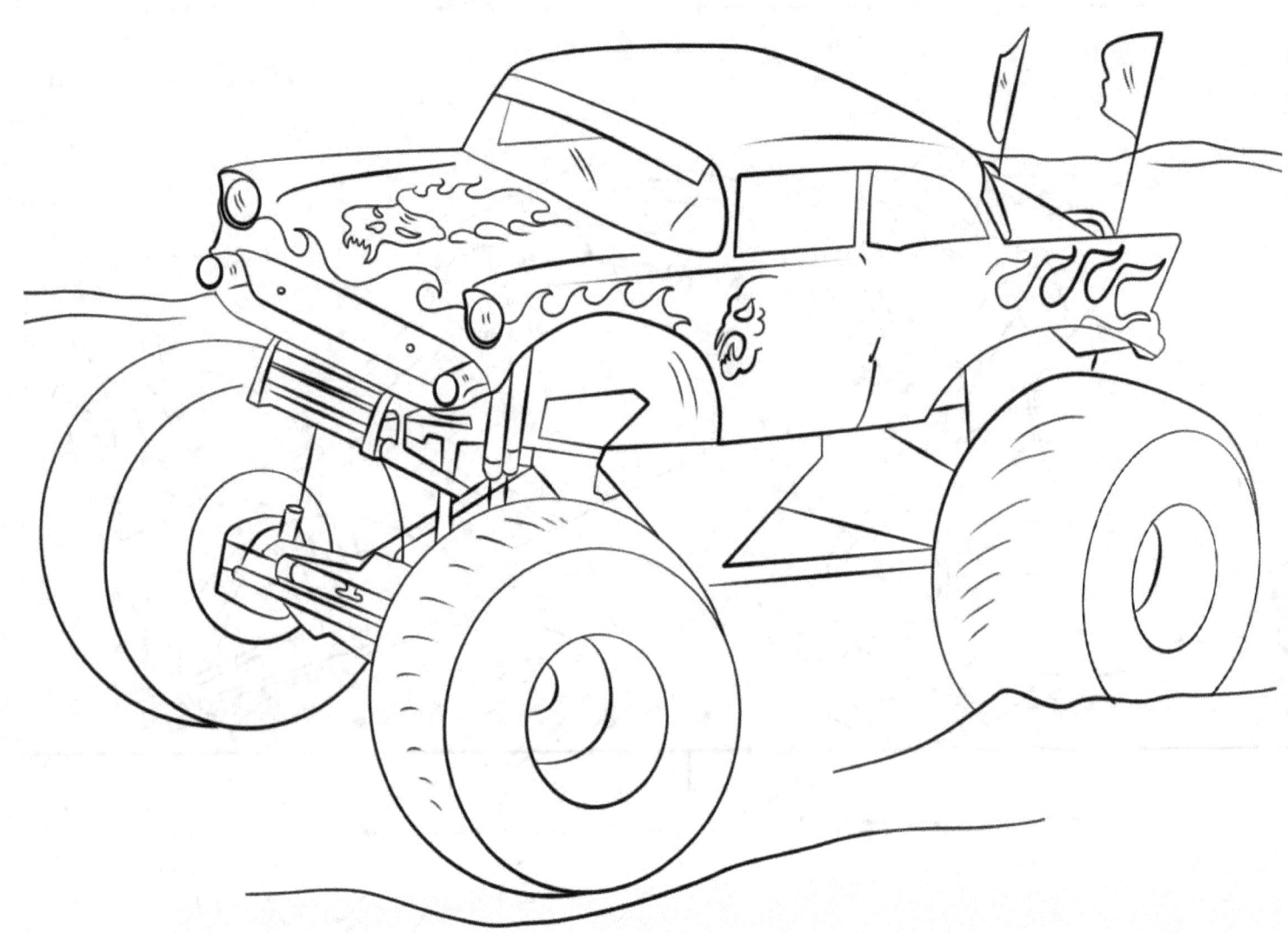

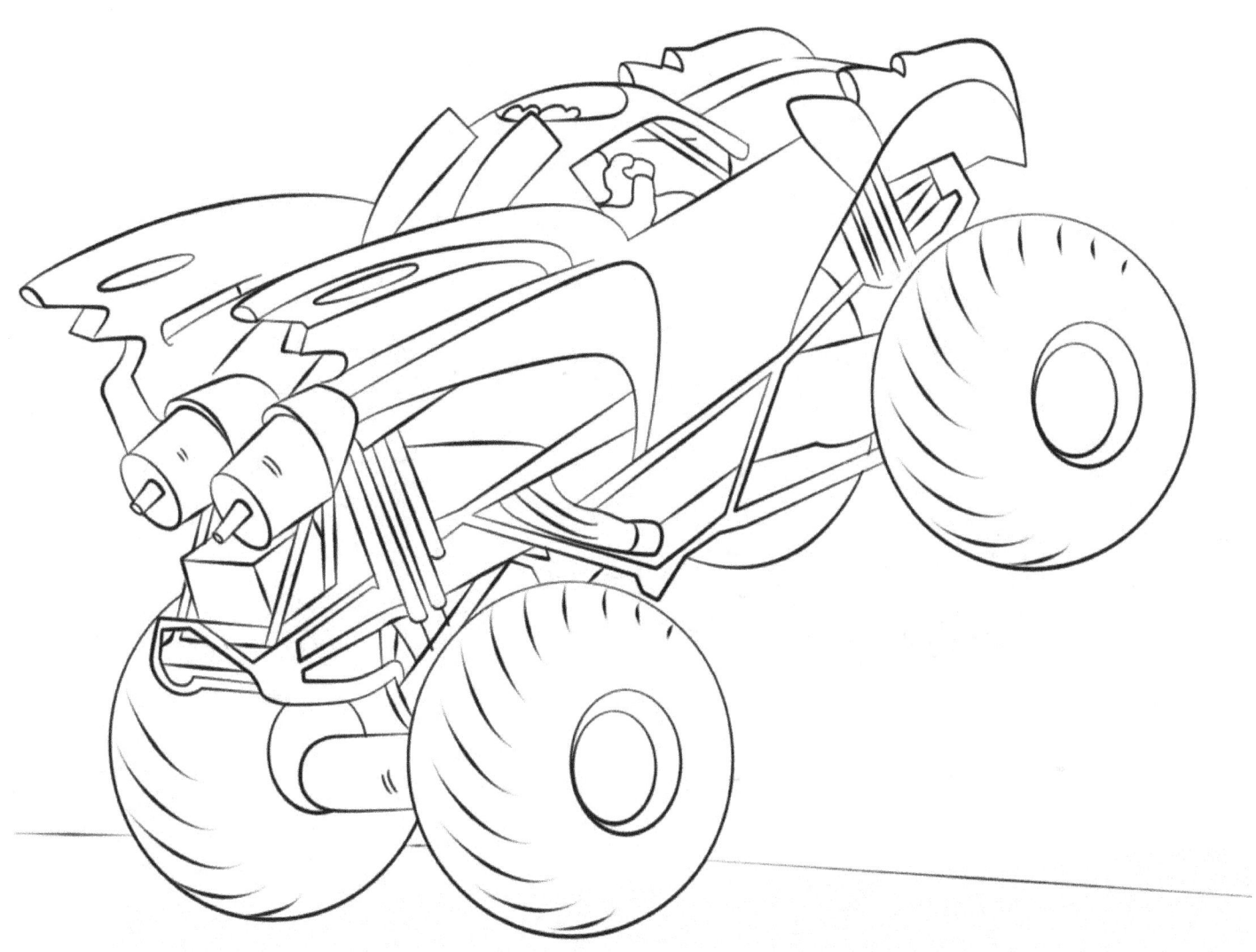

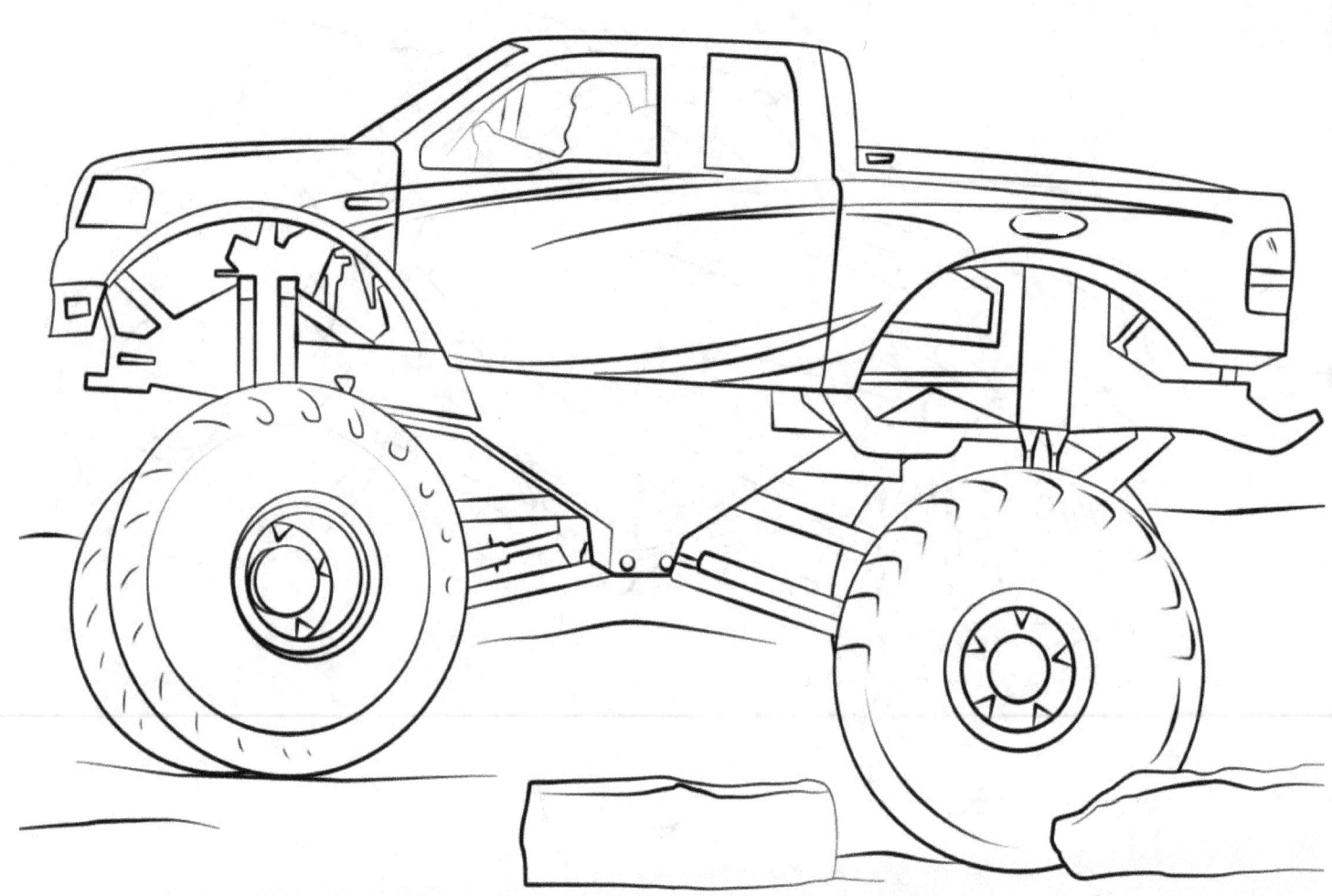

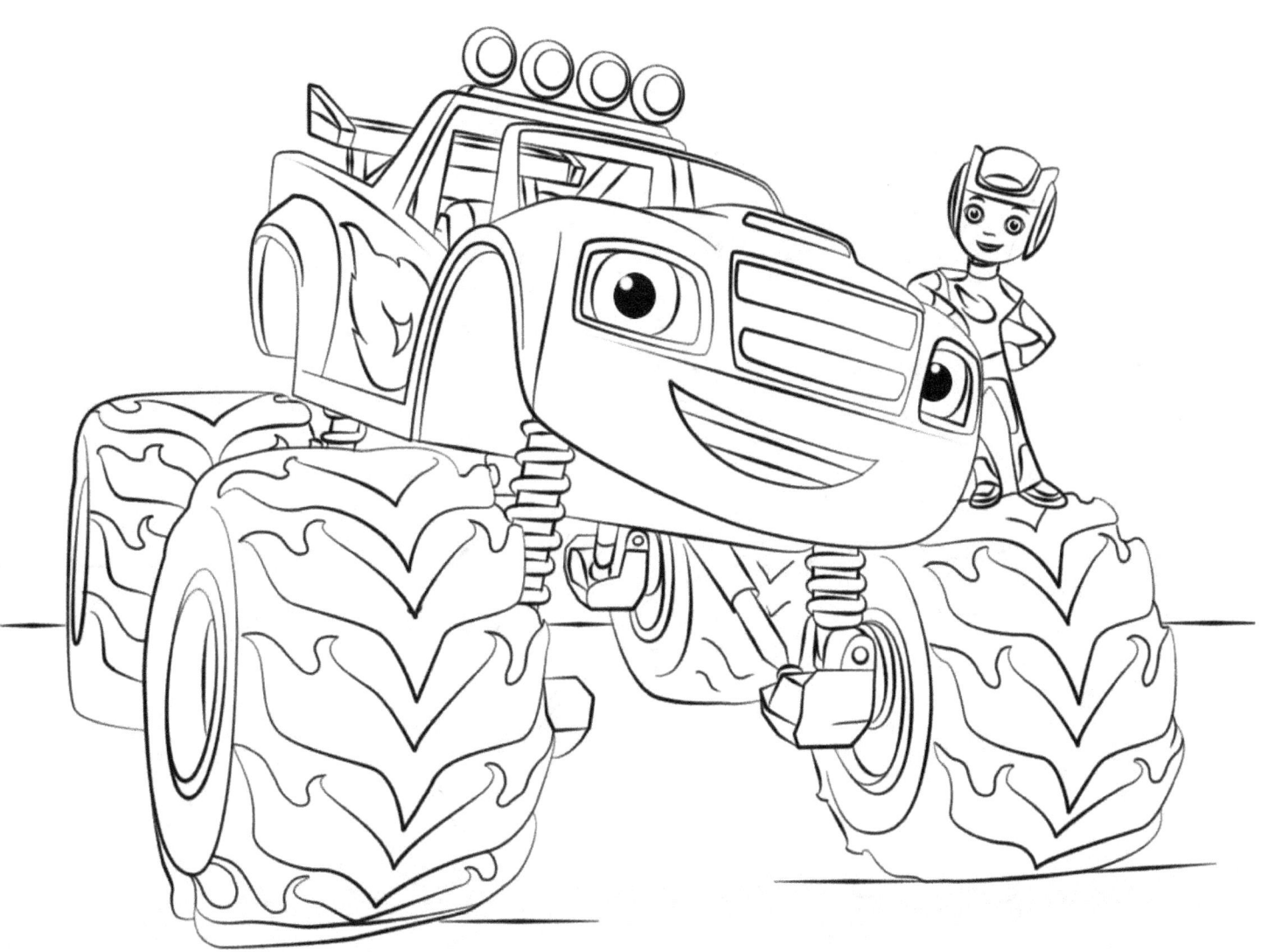

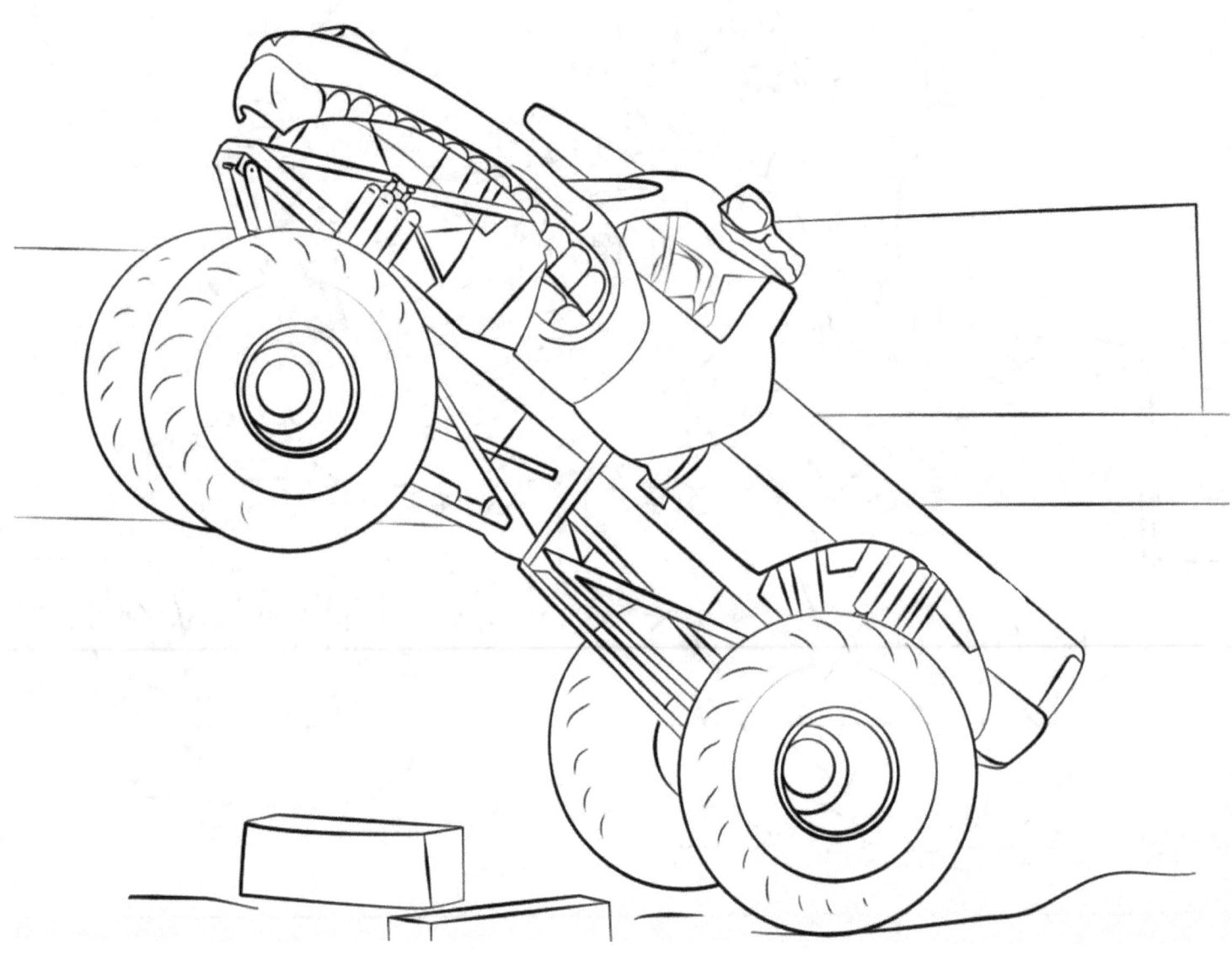

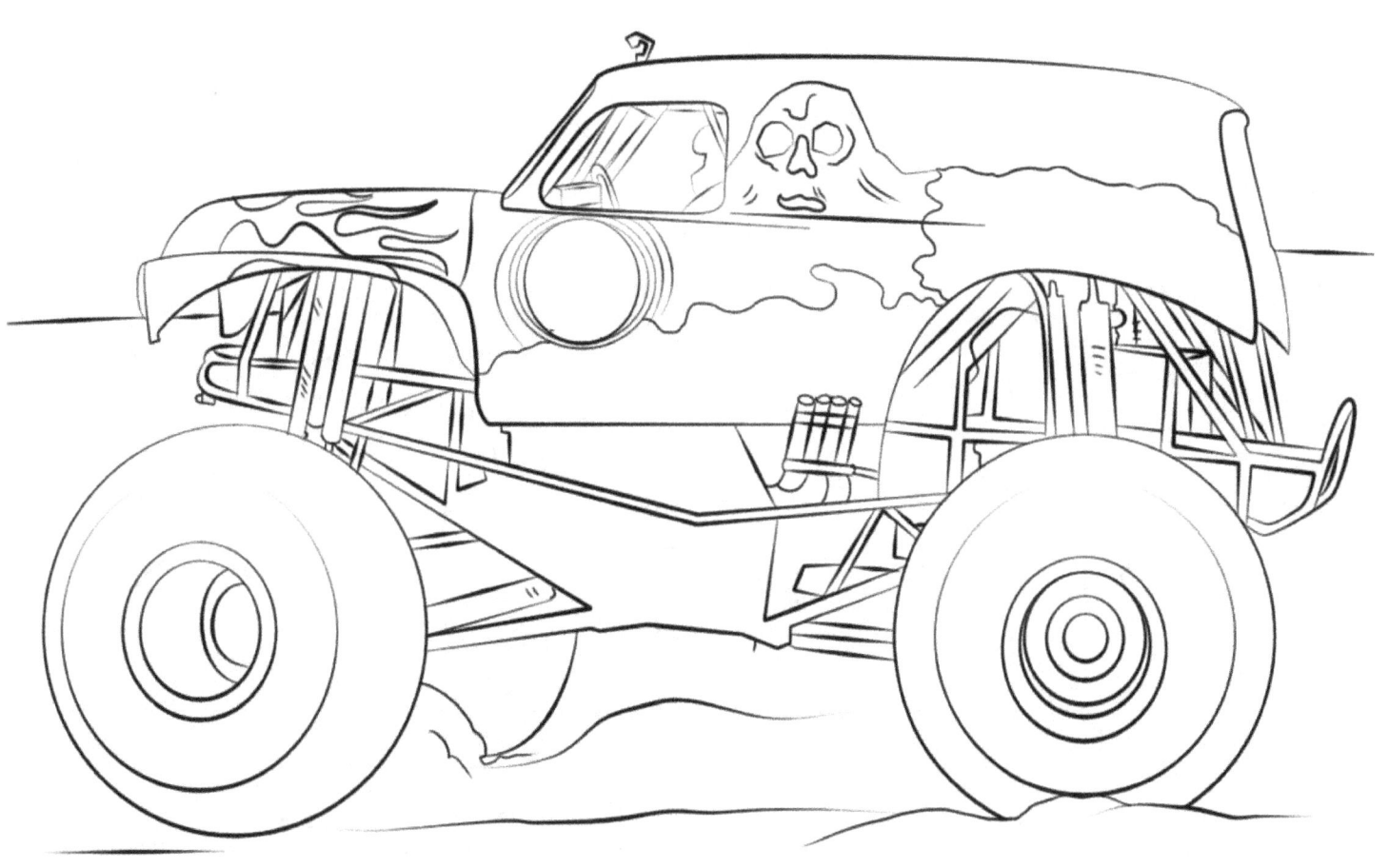

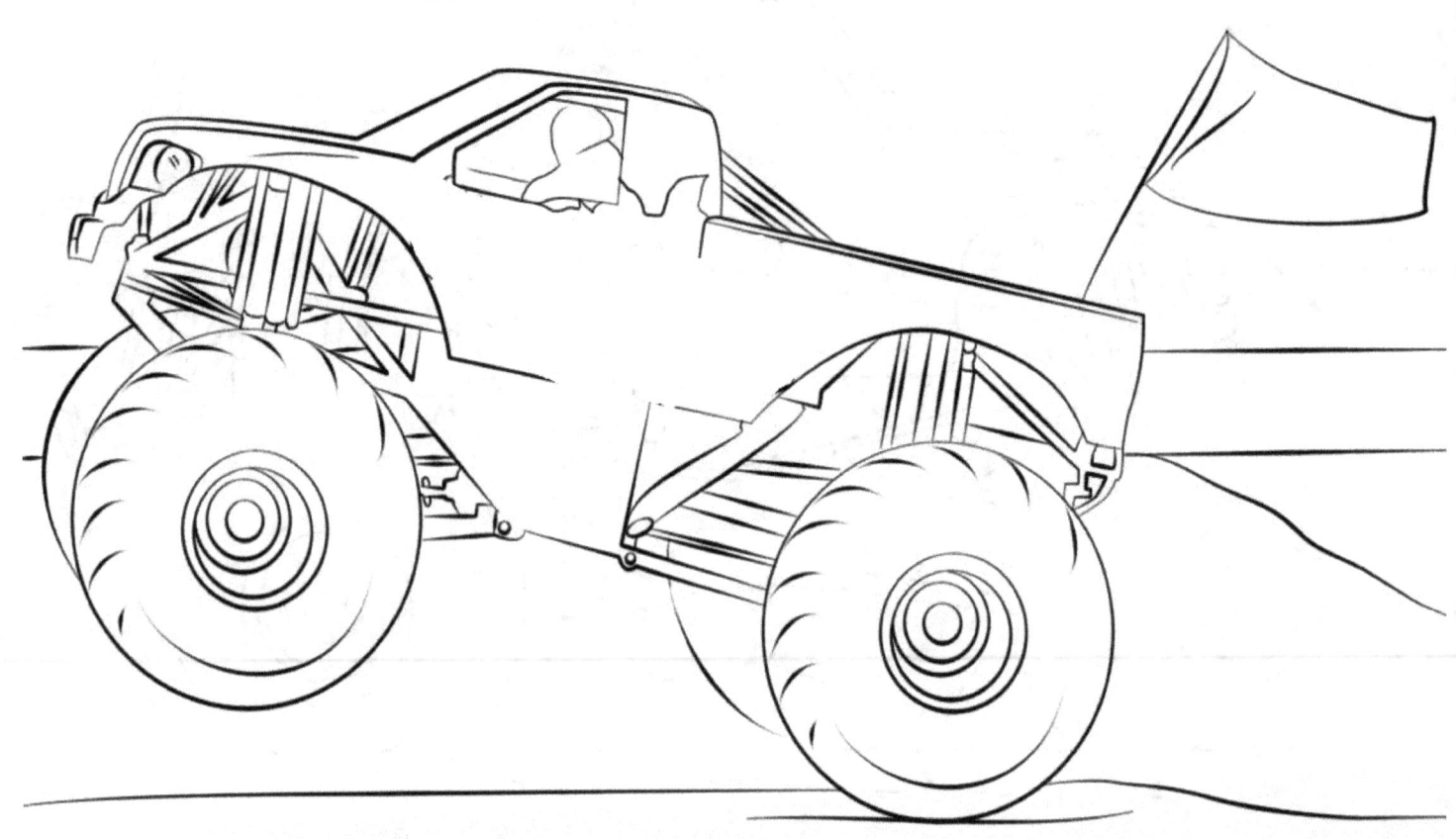

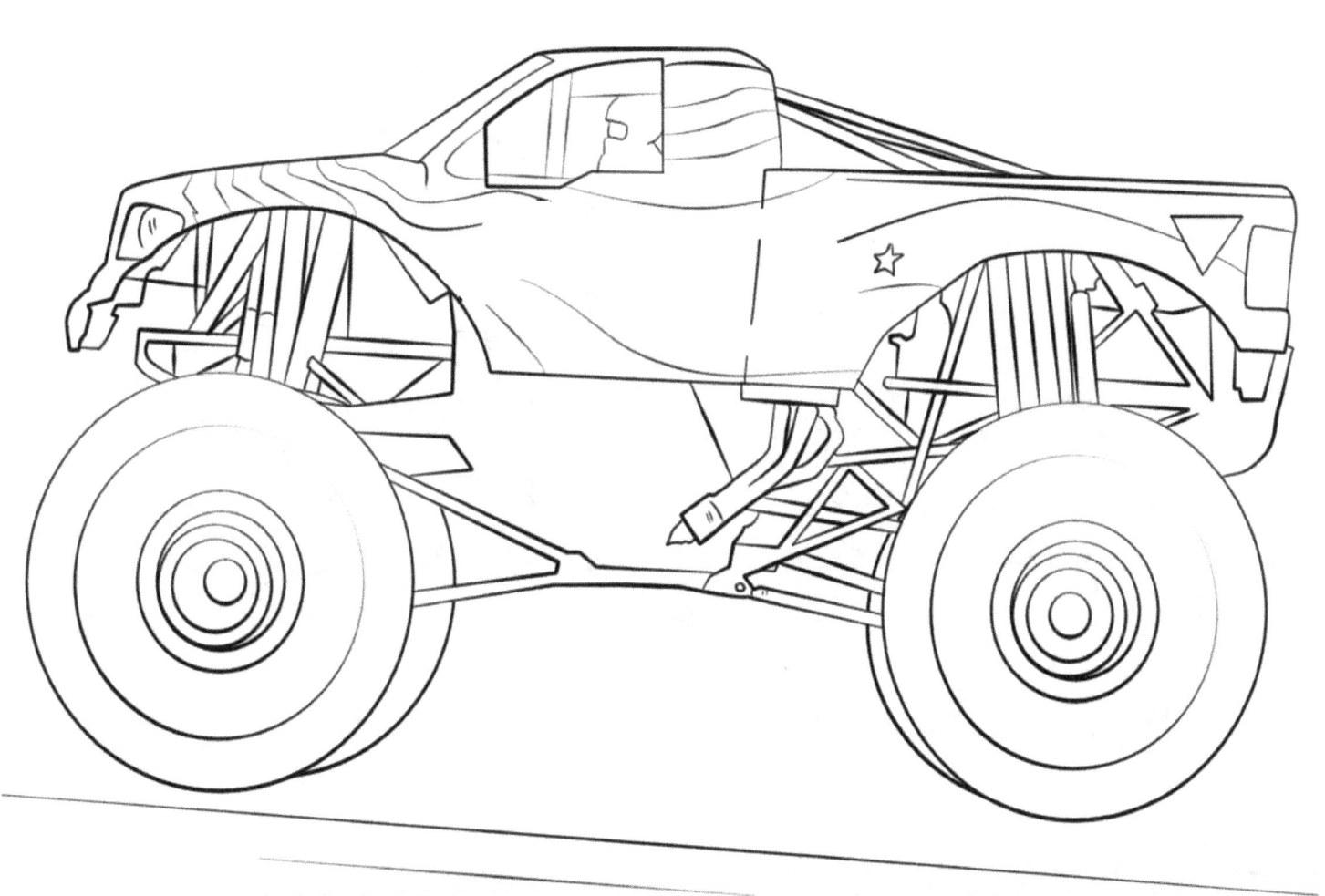

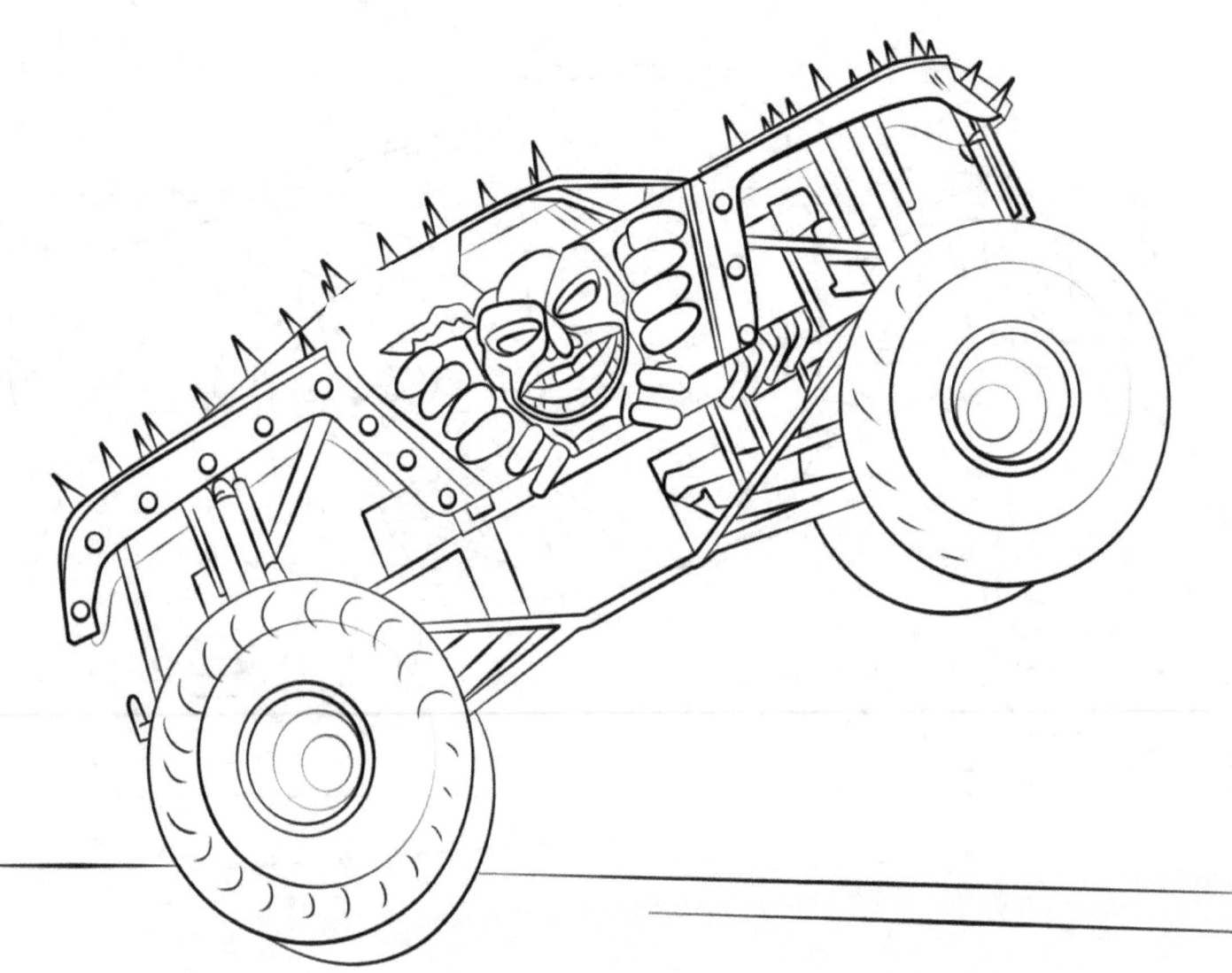

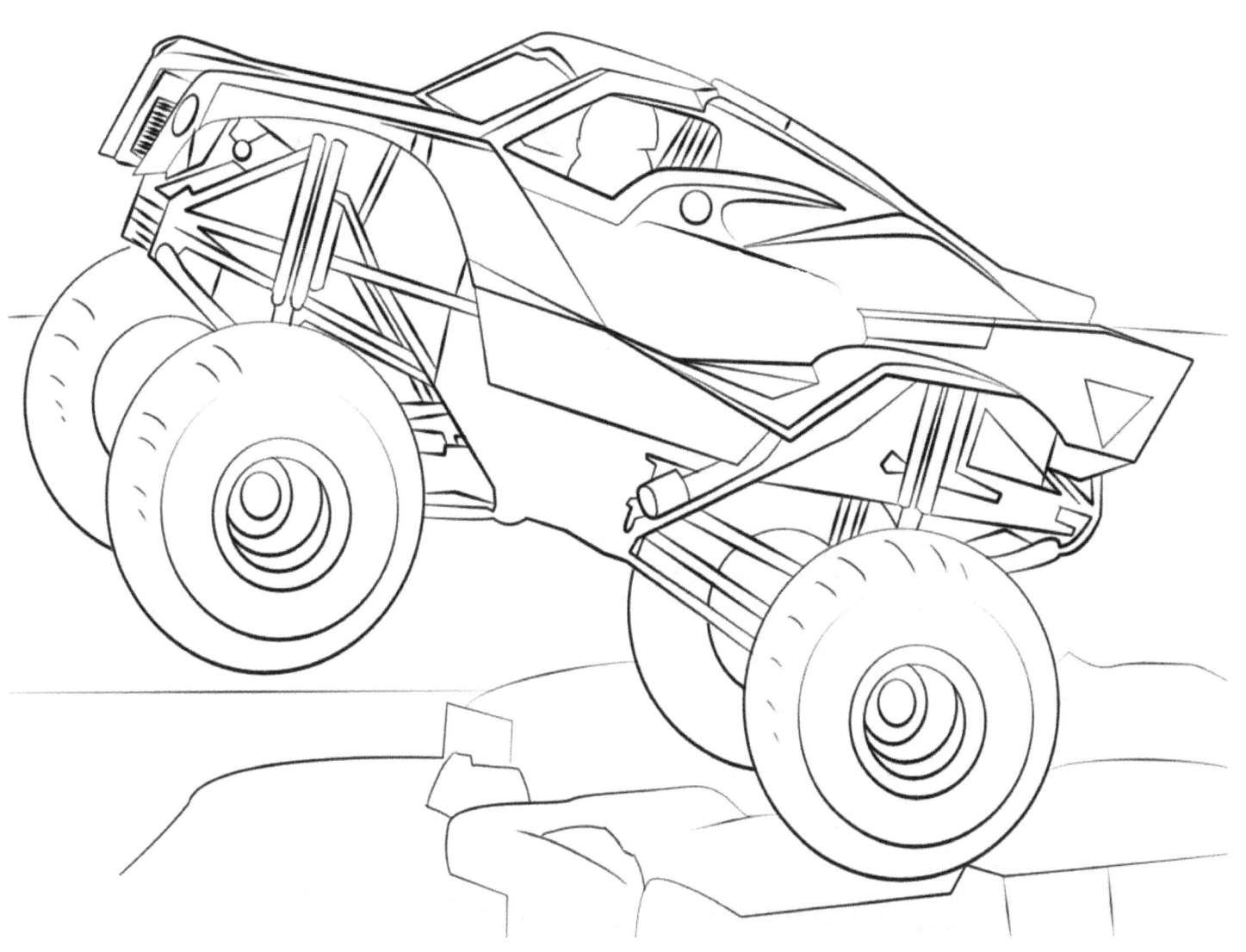

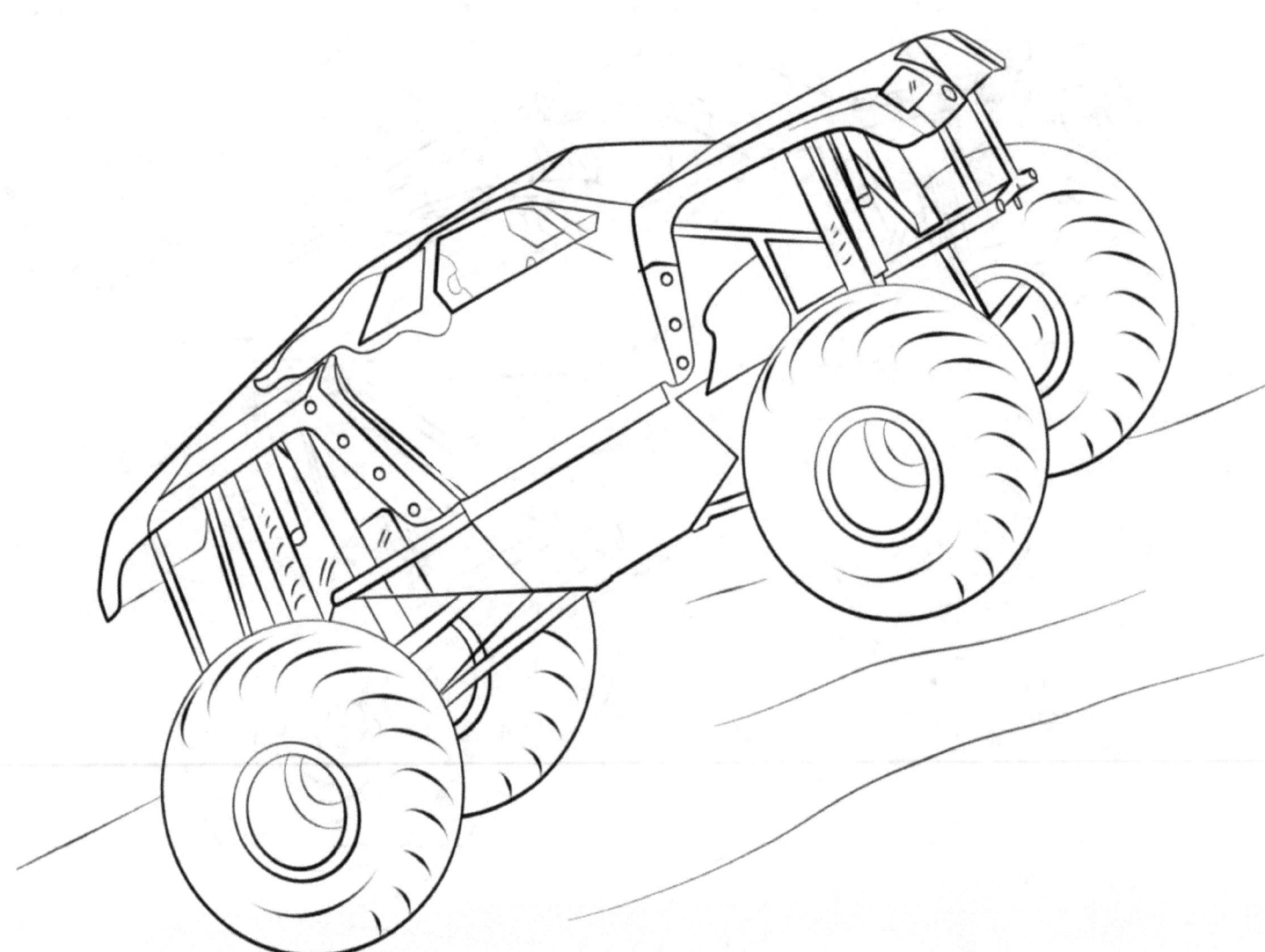

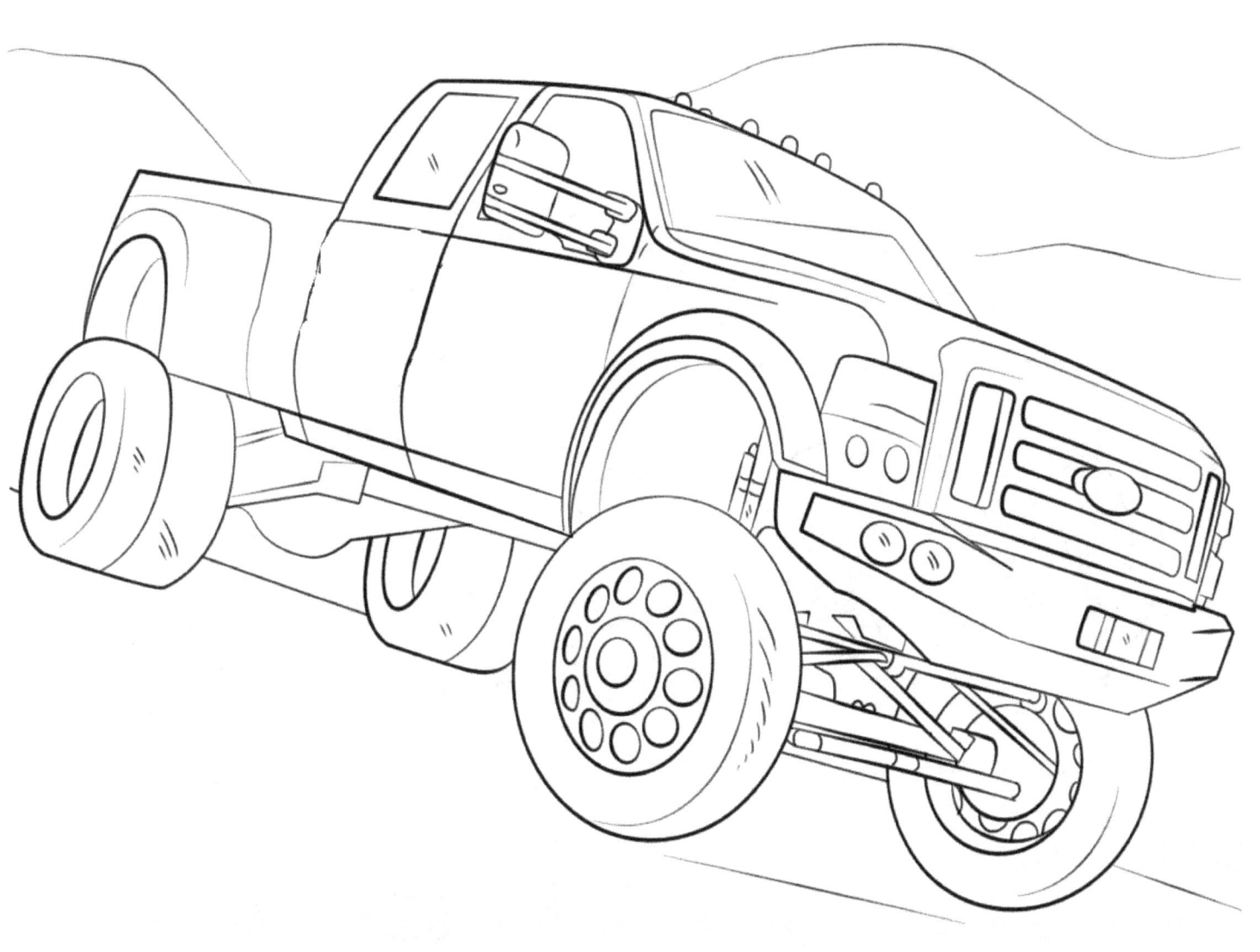

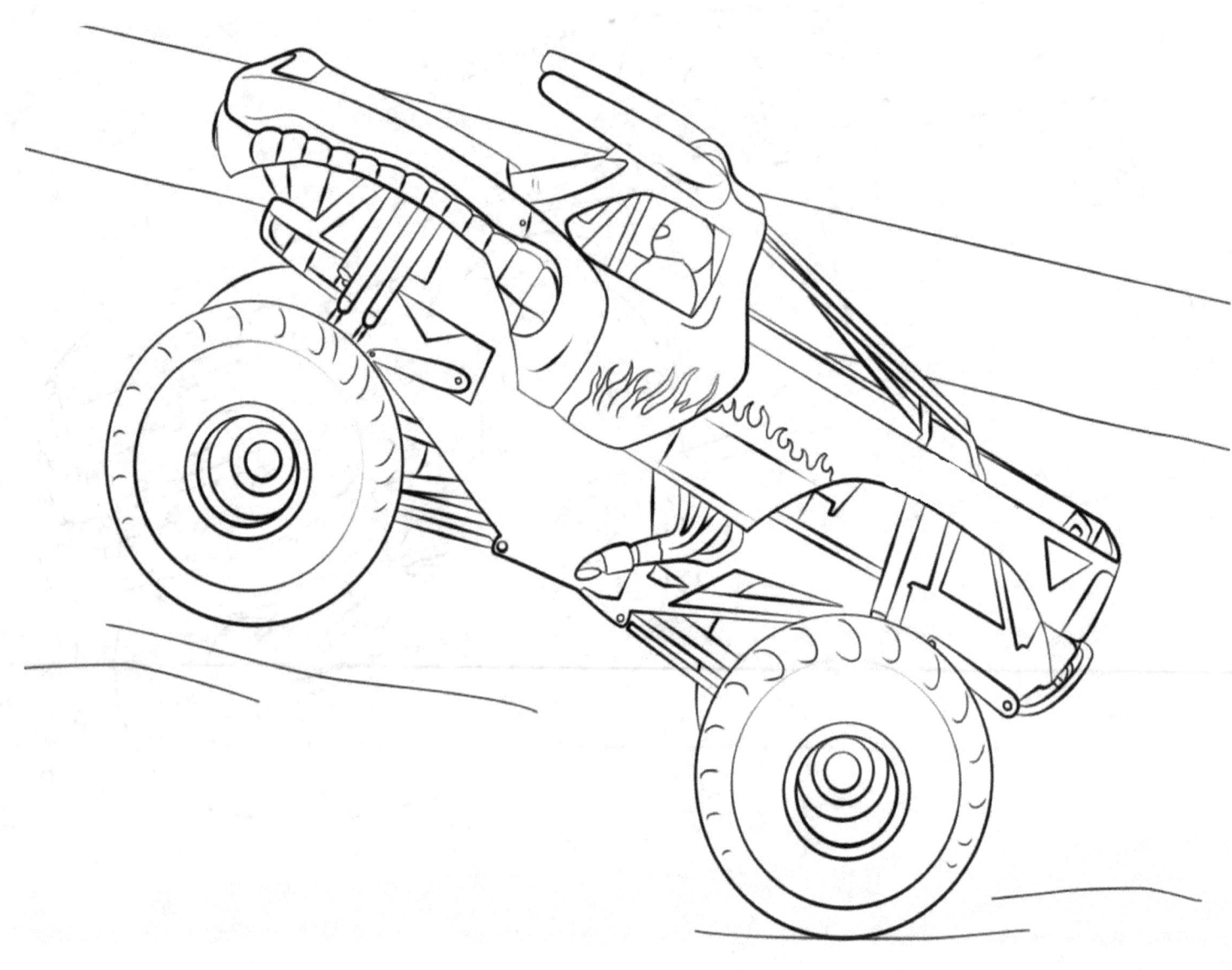

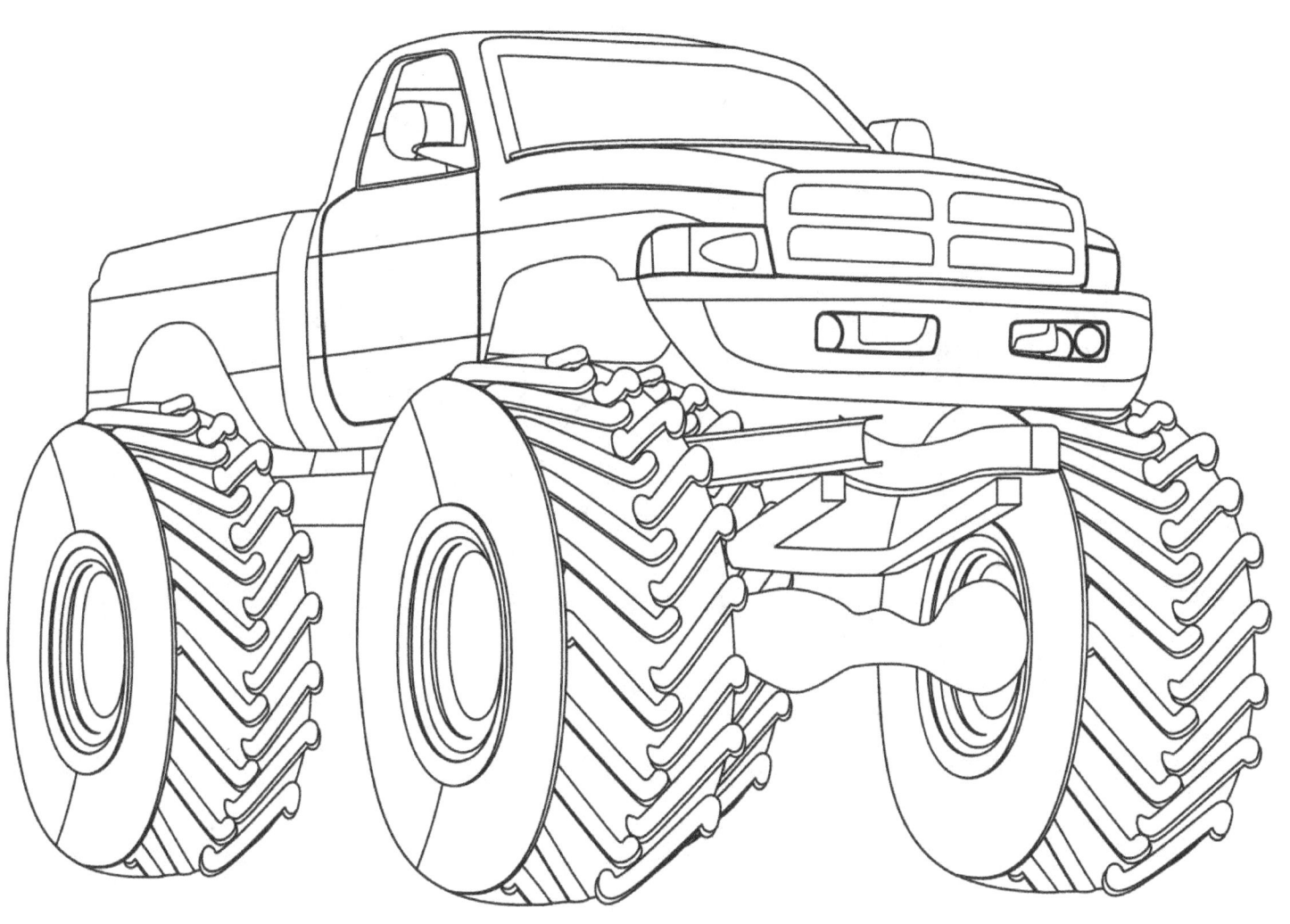

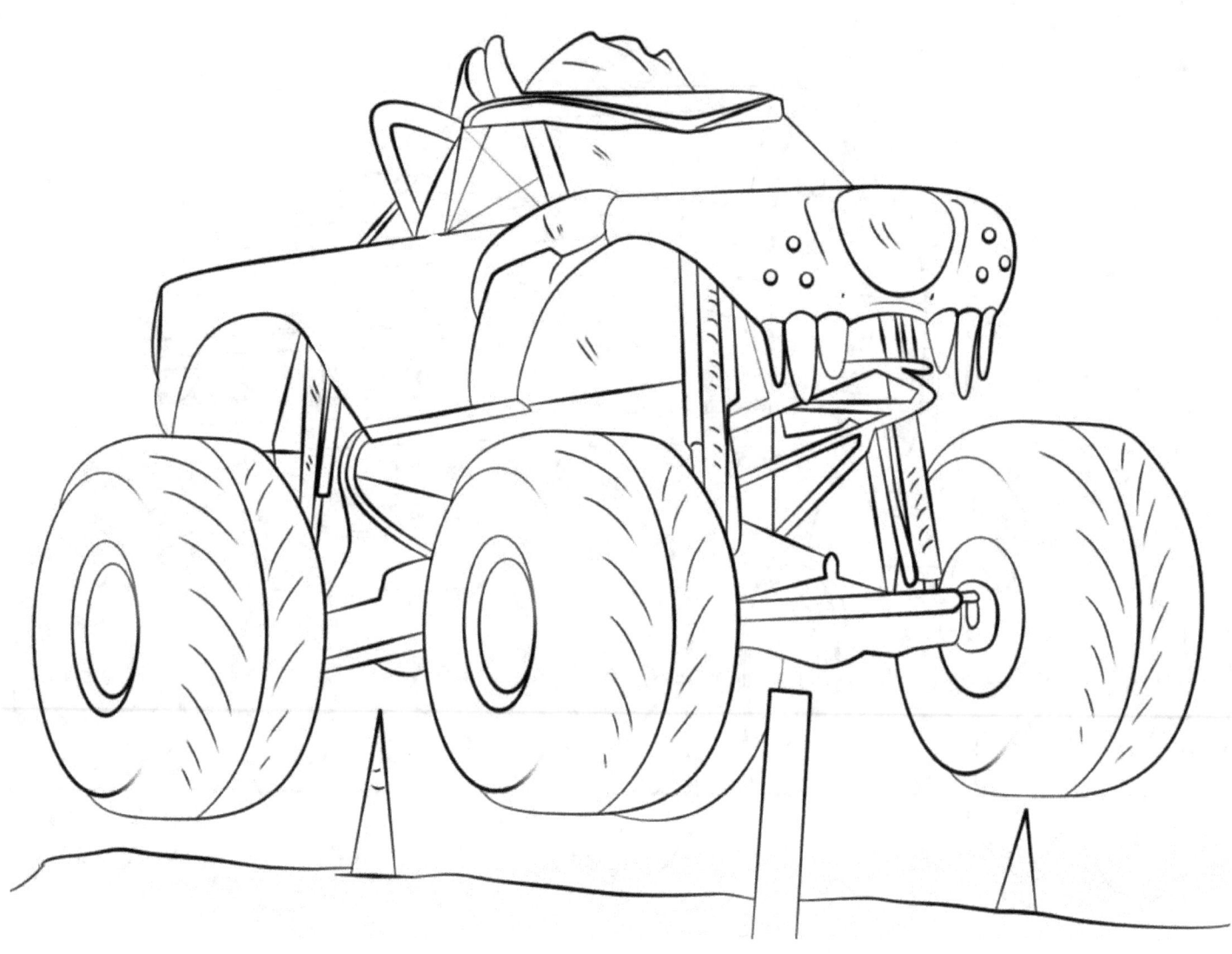

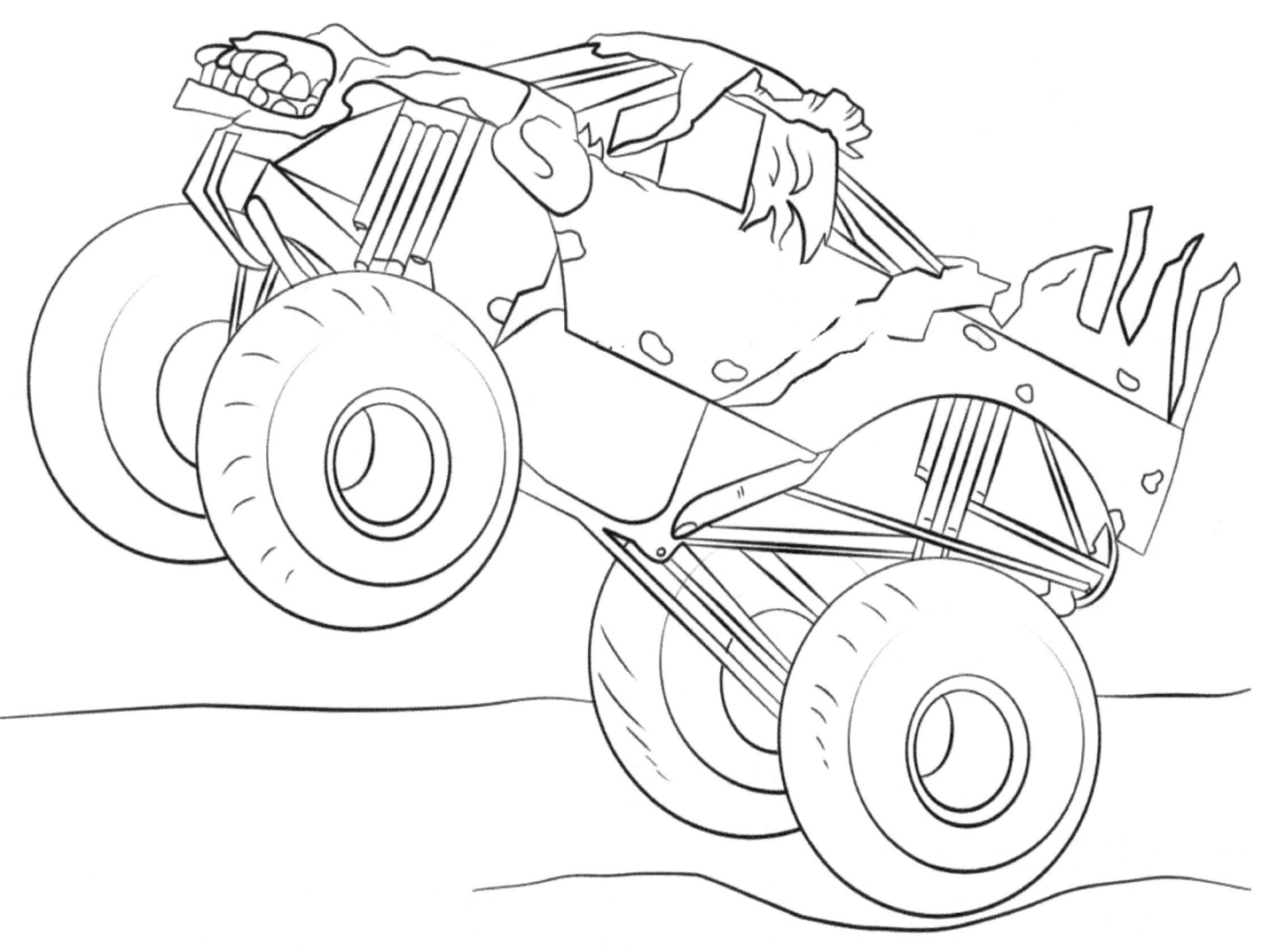

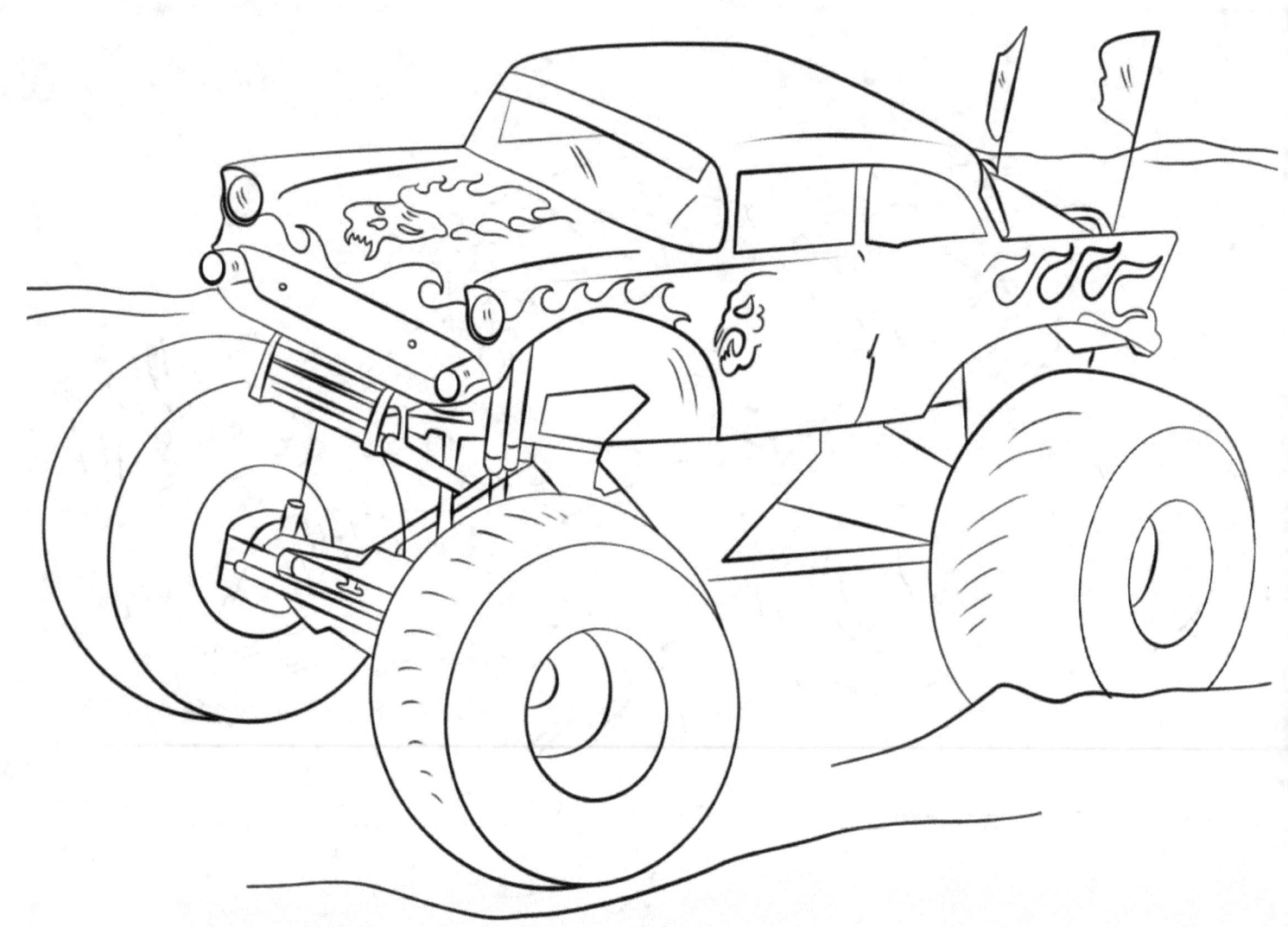

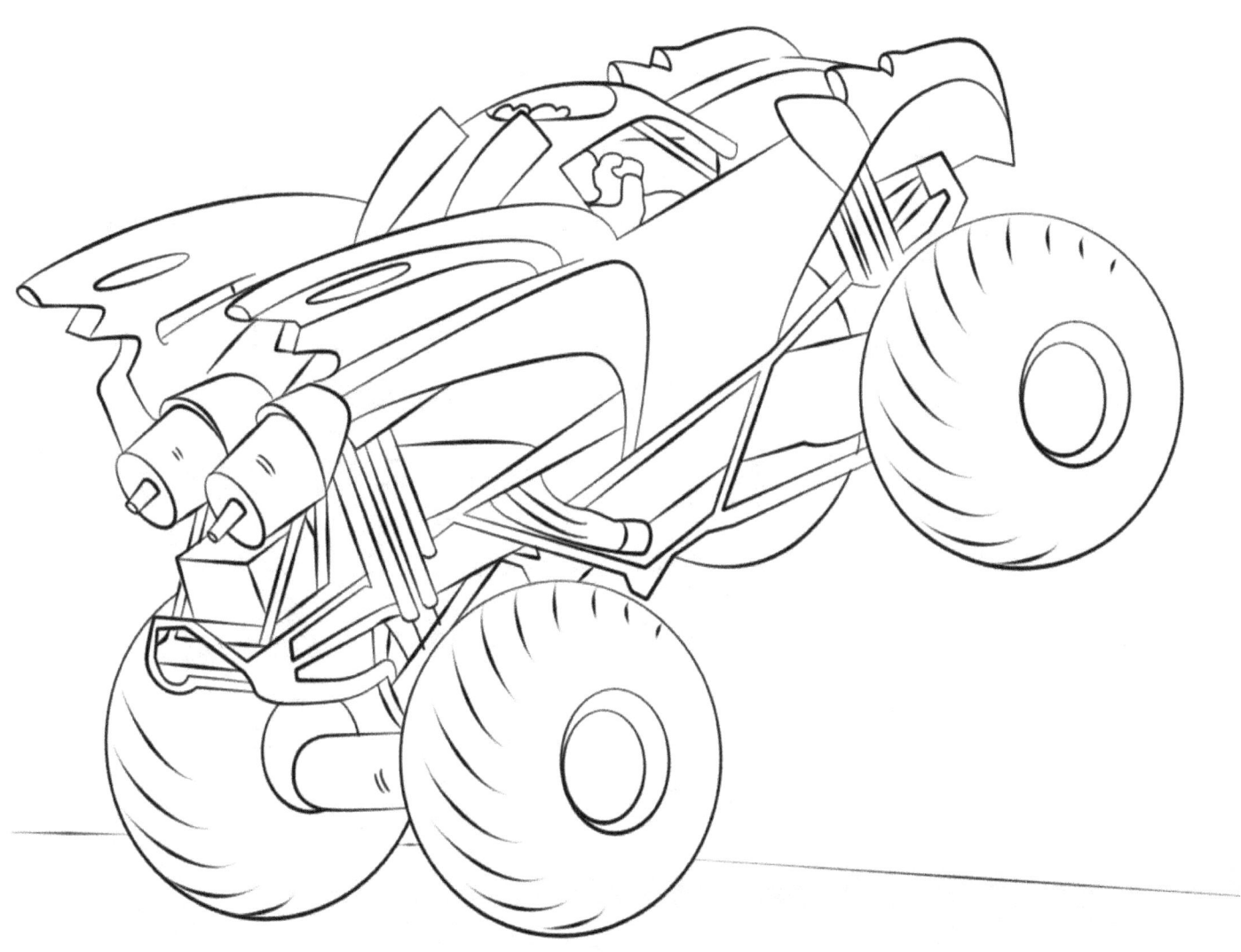

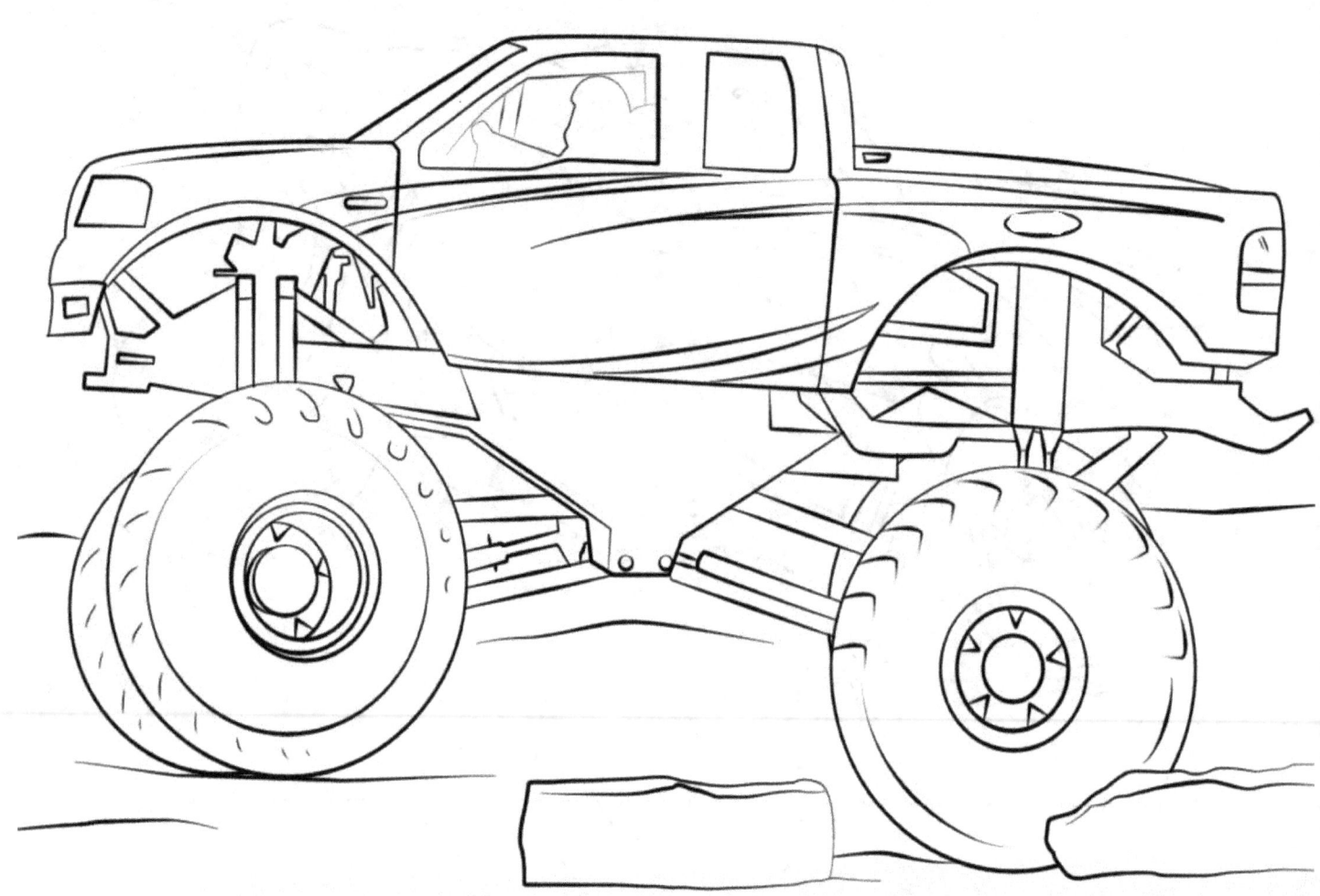

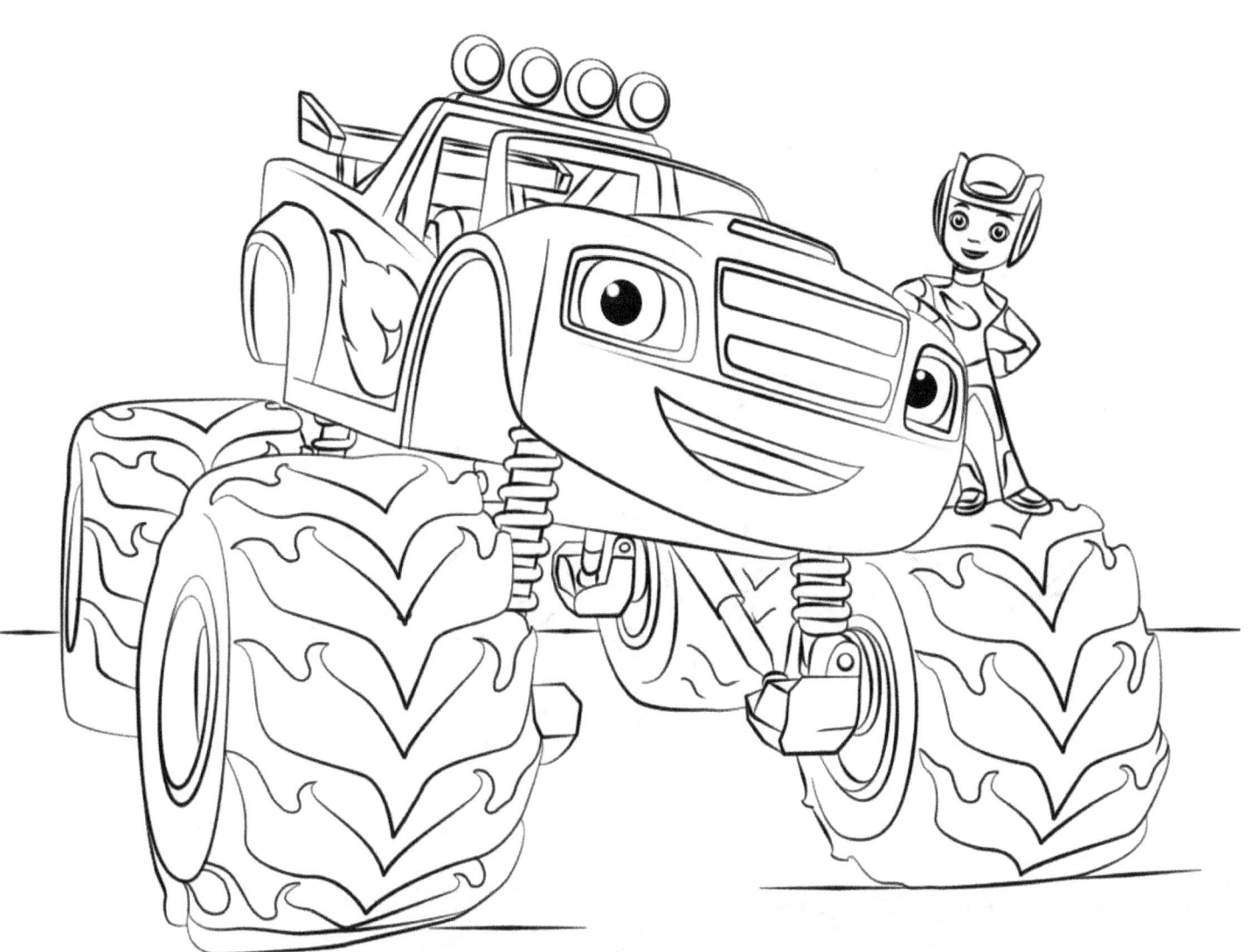

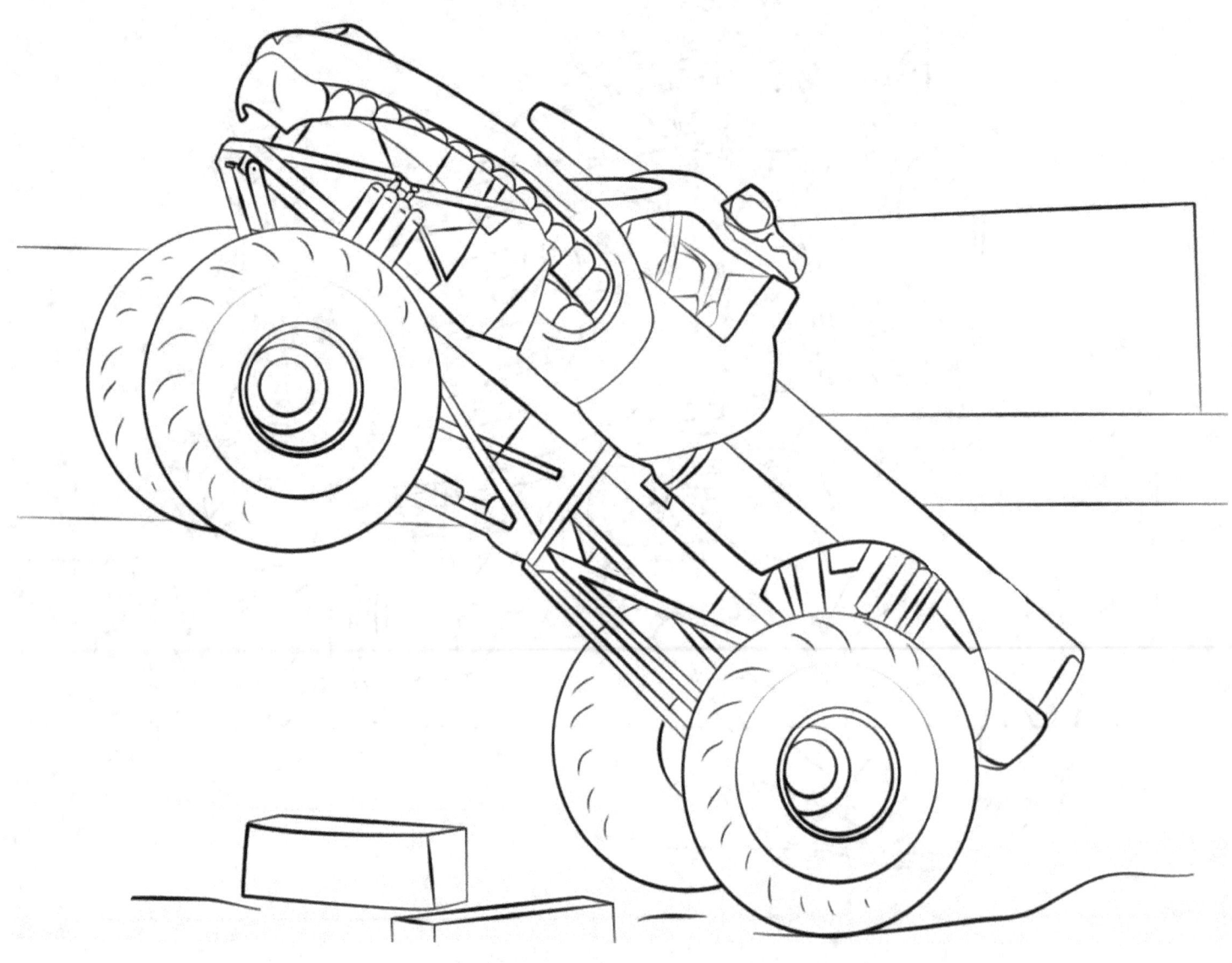

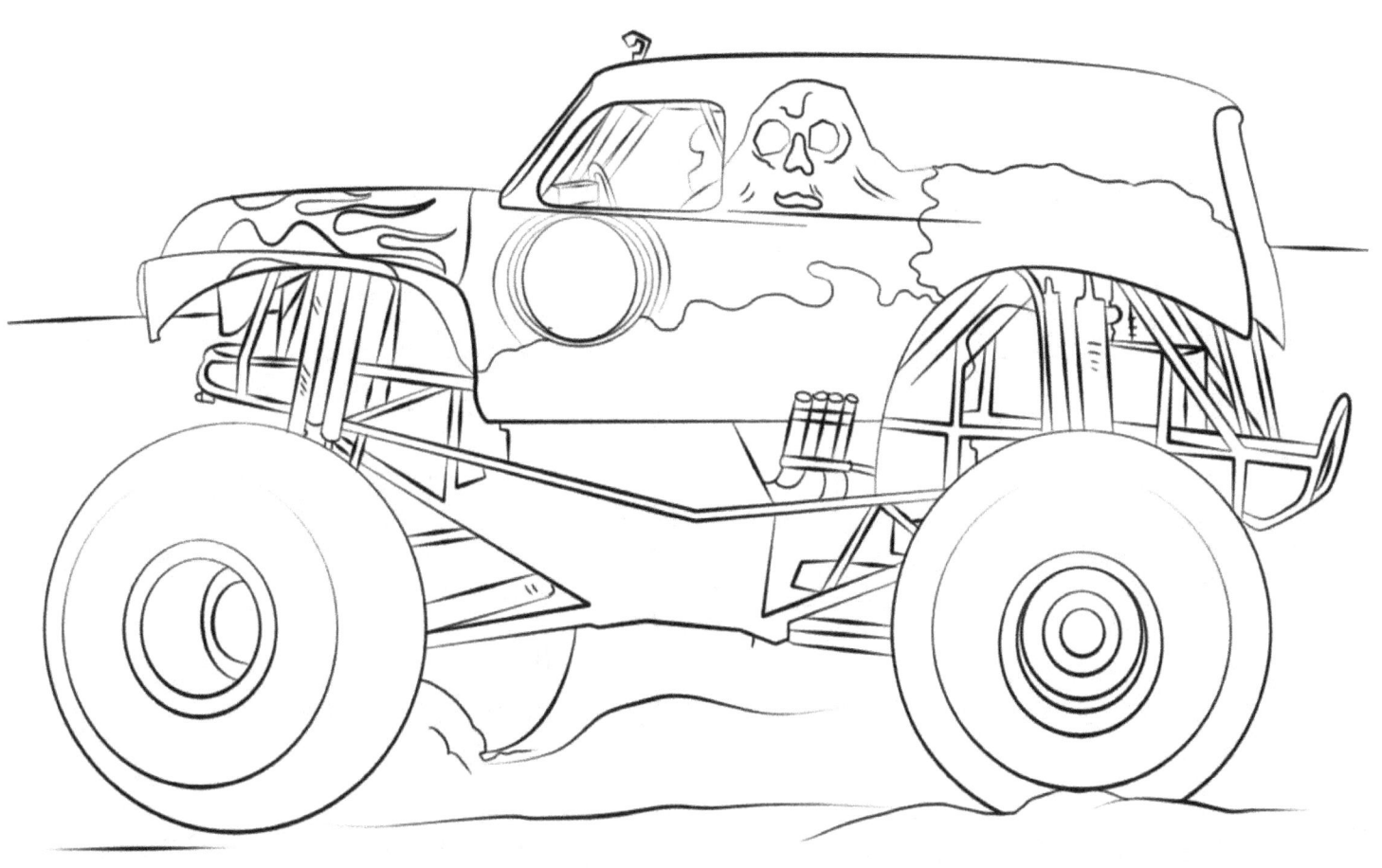

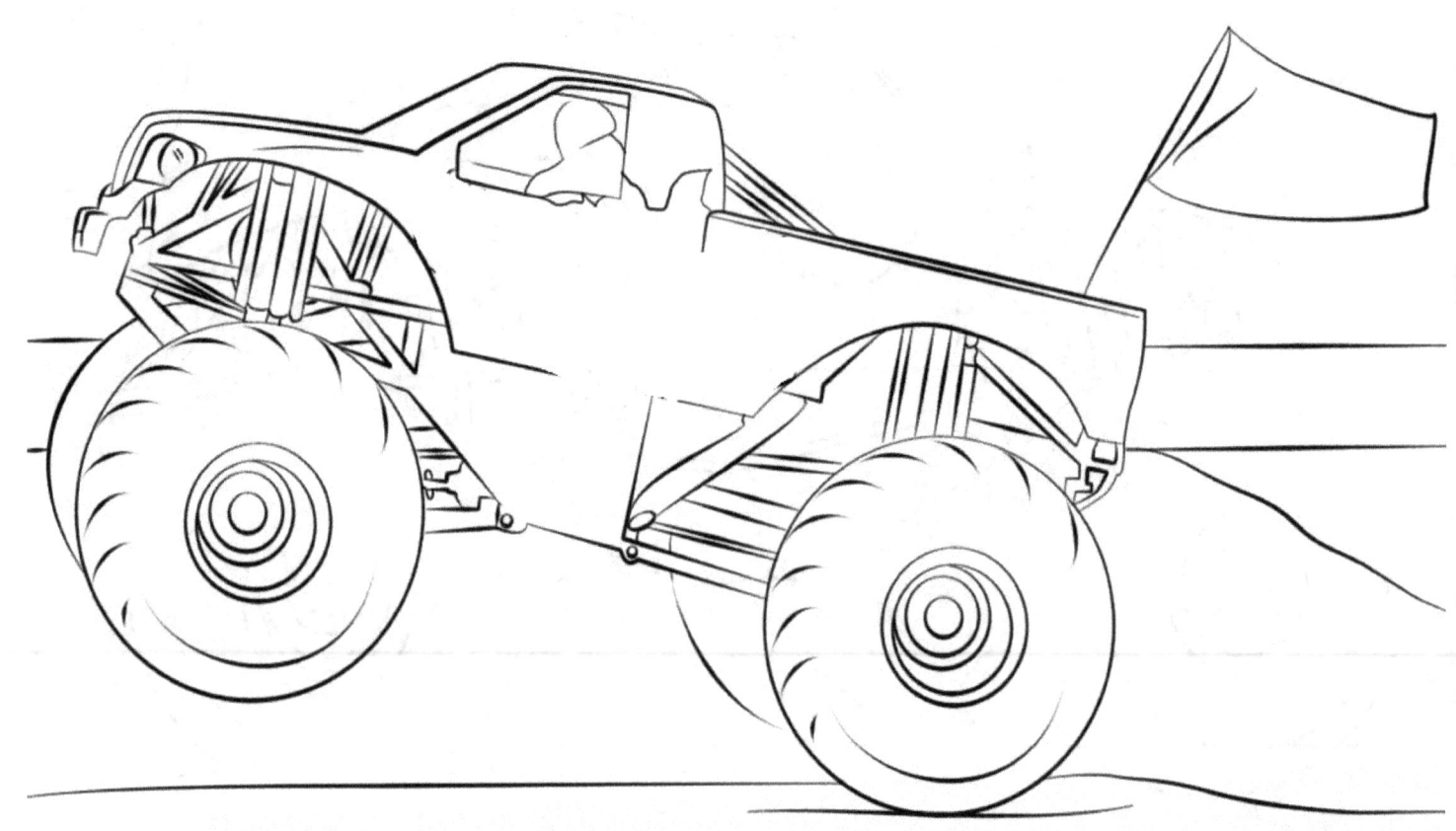

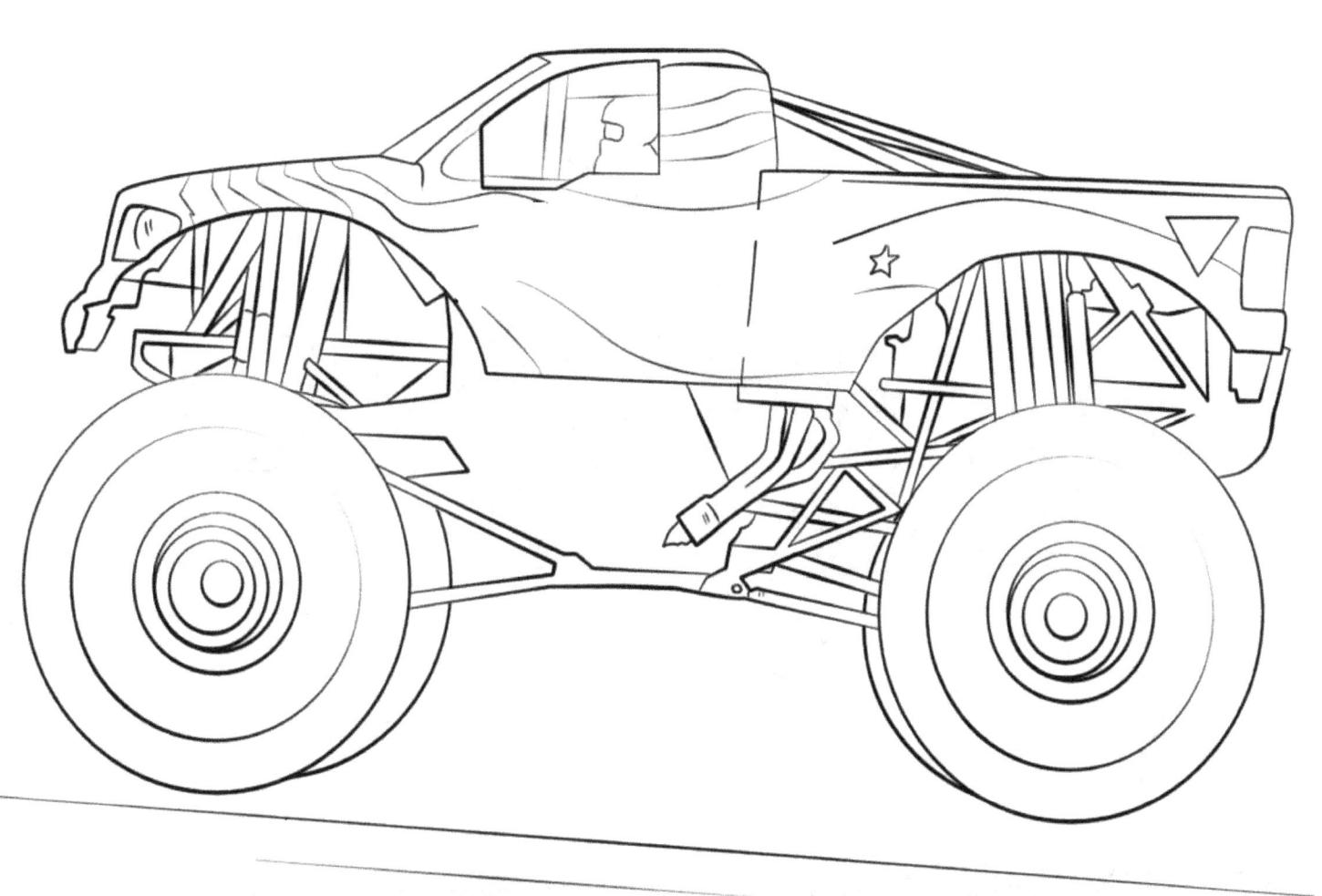

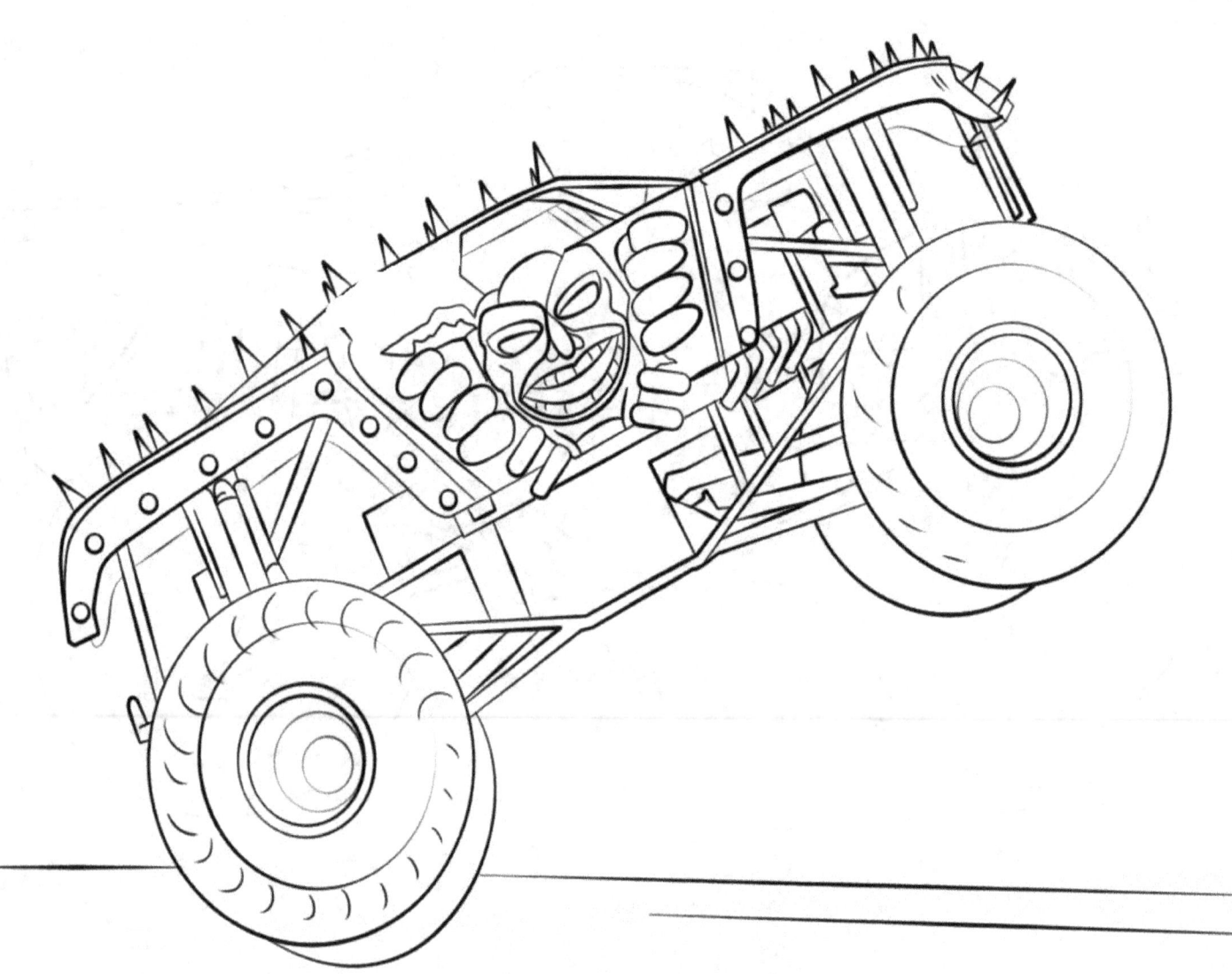

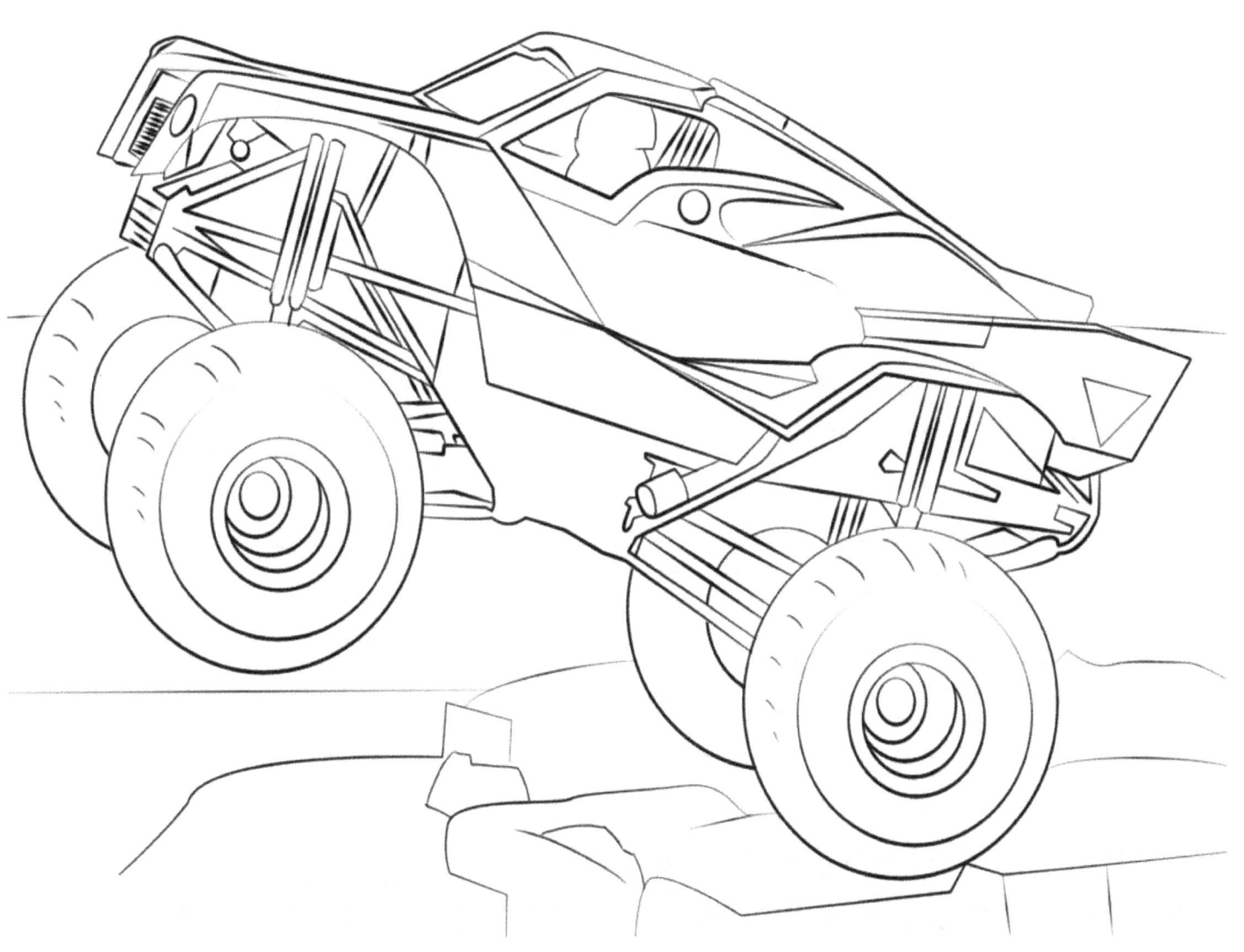

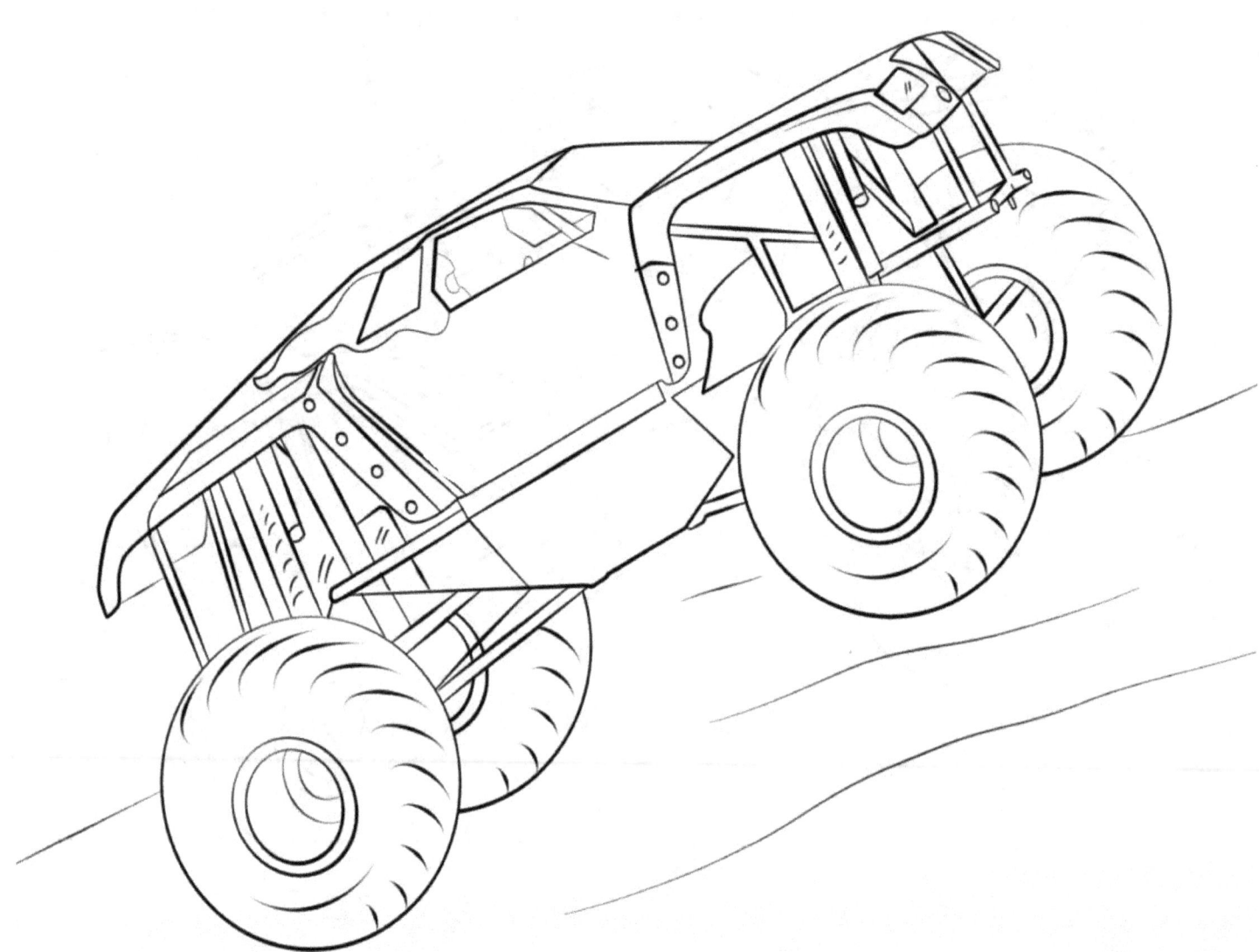

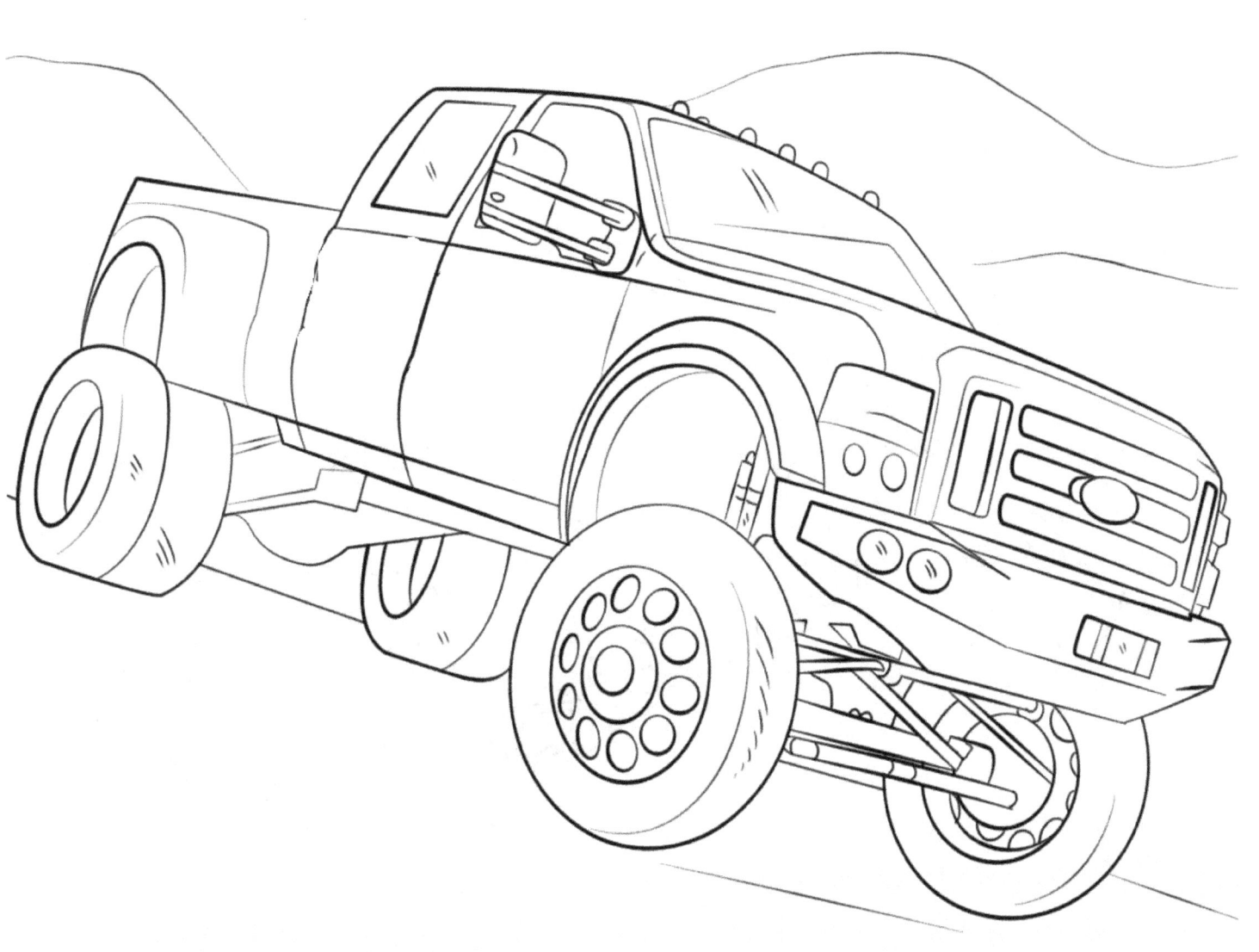

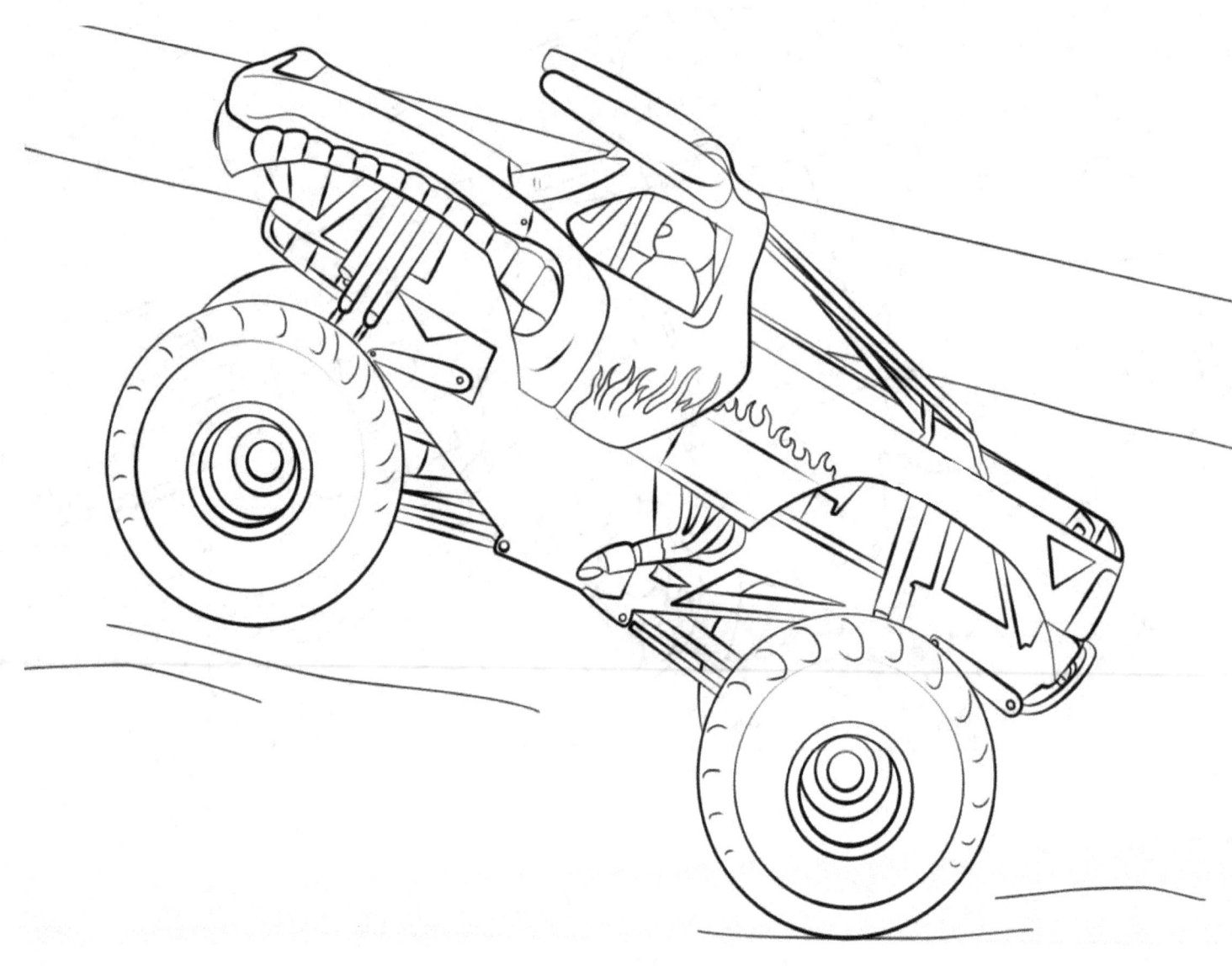

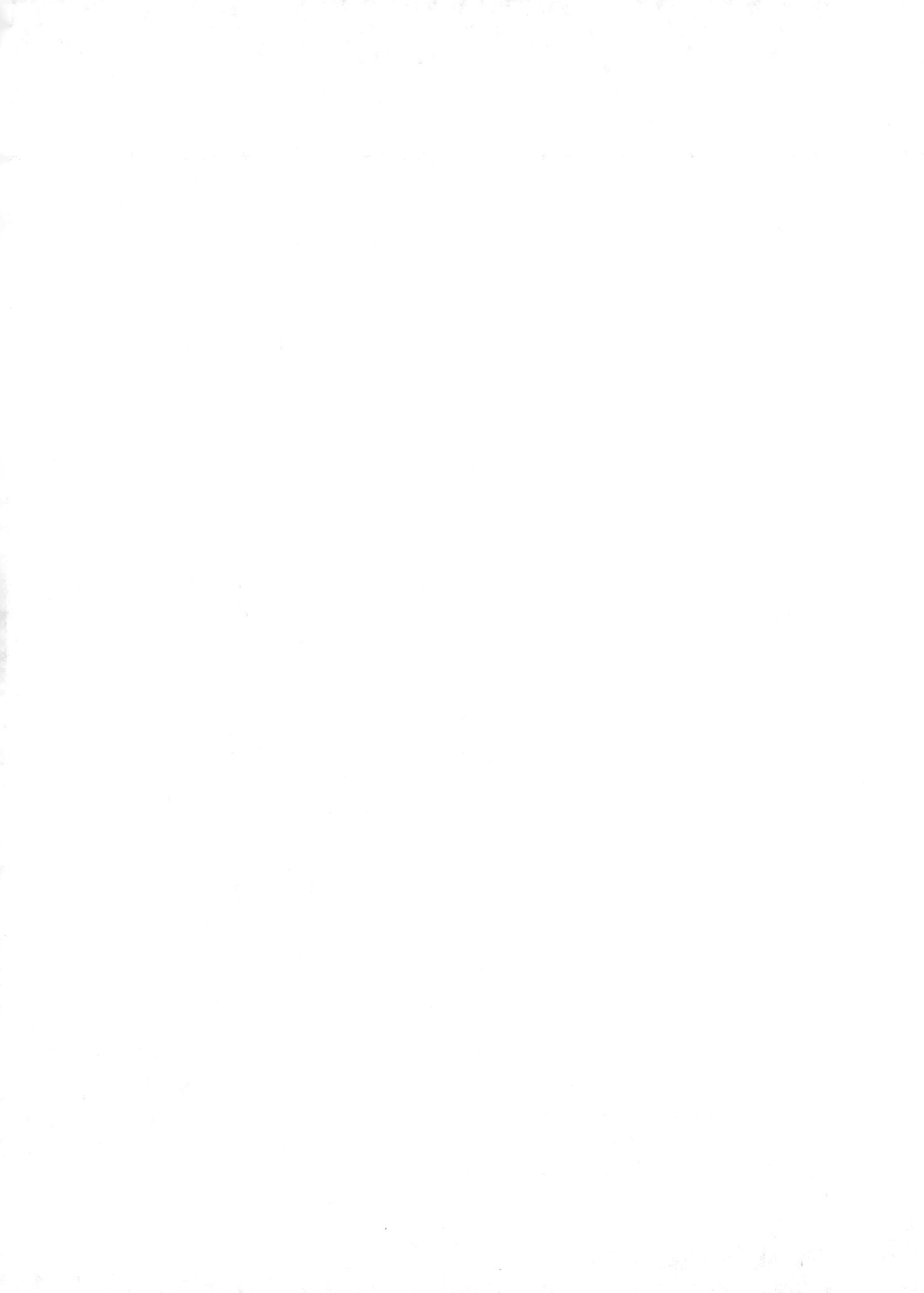

www.ingramcontent.com/pod-product-compliance
Lightning Source LLC
Chambersburg PA
CBHW080443220526
45465CB00007B/2747